Postfoundationalist Reflections in Practical Theology

Postfoundationalist Reflections in Practical Theology

A Framework for a Discipline in Flux

BRIAN C. MACALLAN

Foreword by
JURGENS HENDRIKS

WIPF & STOCK · Eugene, Oregon

POSTFOUNDATIONALIST REFLECTIONS IN PRACTICAL THEOLOGY
A Framework for a Discipline in Flux

Copyright © 2014 Brian C. Macallan. All rights reserved. Except for brief quotations in critical publications or reviews, no part of this book may be reproduced in any manner without prior written permission from the publisher. Write: Permissions, Wipf and Stock Publishers, 199 W. 8th Ave., Suite 3, Eugene, OR 97401.

Wipf & Stock
An Imprint of Wipf and Stock Publishers
199 W. 8th Ave., Suite 3
Eugene, OR 97401

www.wipfandstock.com

ISBN 13: 978-1-62032-815-6

Manufactured in the U.S.A.

06/03/2014

Contents

Foreword by Jurgens Hendriks   vii

Acknowledgements   ix

ONE   Introduction   1

TWO   Foundationalism Explored   13

THREE   Practical Theology   35

FOUR   A Postfoundationalist Practical Theology   69

FIVE   Conclusion   159

Bibliography   163

Foreword

An old world is dying and with it the relics of a church and its theology too. The new world that is born is dangerously unstable but excitingly free and inviting.

This book is a diary with field notes of the adventurous journey of the church, of theology, and of a follower of Jesus Christ through the liminal sphere of the transition between the old and new world.

In the old world church and theology was caught by the hubris of the illusion that fallible humans can have absolute knowledge and certainty, can actually solve whatever problem they are confronted with. This certainty is described by the word *foundationalism*. It was born during the Enlightenment and reared in modernity. *Fundamentalism* is its rather ugly offspring, the bitter fruits from which nobody can escape.

The philosophical manger of post-foundationalism is described by a practical theologian. Practical theology was born in the liminal space between paradigms. Thus the research question of the book is whether practical theology has moved beyond the foundationalist assumptions of the previous era. The other side of the coin is the aim of the book: to guide practical theology to be free from the shackles of foundationalism and its offspring fundamentalism. As such, it is defining practical theology, describing its journey as it endeavors to discover its true postfoundationalist identity.

The book narrates the story of practical theology. Its identity is a humble one because of the old paradigm in which it is born and rather hesitantly welcomed. However, practical theology is no longer insecure with an unstable identity. When the discipline came of age it was focusing on the triune God from which all wisdom and mercy flows. It knows about its fallibility and therefore acknowledges that it needs community. This community is not only that of its theology brothers and sisters, but also of all who endeavor to find the light. It is at peace within a global scientific

Foreword

community because it knows its own identity well and it certainly has a contribution to make.

One of the most valuable aspects of this book is the way in which it helps one escape the fear of relativism. As a missional practical theology it has a calling, a vocation, a dream. There is an alternative future and it has a crucial role to play because its identity as a discipline is inherently transformative. It is not shy to cross boundaries and be in dialogue with other disciplines. It actually realizes it can't go alone.

Like Abraham of old the author of this book lived through the journey that he describes. It's his life story. As such, the book is like the tree Abraham planted at Beersheba (Gen 21:33); it will give shade to all of us who are on the same journey. It is an altar like the ones Abraham built because of very real encounters with God. Simply to visit these altars will strengthen us.

This new world and the new understanding of doing theology unlock the future for God's people, the church, and the world. Hope is a reality when we realize the kingdom of God is at hand and becomes visible and tangible on the missional journey. Being in a post-foundational paradigm reminds us that *we* need not be the foundation. Thus we are simultaneously free, secure, and called.

Jurgens Hendriks
Stellenbosch, South Africa, October 2013

Acknowledgements

The journey of this book goes a long way. From its beginnings in Stellenbosch in South Africa to Amsterdam in the Netherlands, and finally to Melbourne in Australia. Amidst all the change and difficulty, my doctoral supervisor Jurgens Hendriks, previous professor of Practical Theology at Stellenbosch, has been the constant encouragement and support that kept me on the goal. His constant faith in my work, wisdom, and direction have made this possible. My co-supervisor professor Ian Nell, who came in at a critical juncture of the journey, spent many hours challenging me to widen and deepen my sources. His sharp critique was given as he believed in the importance of the work and the material I was engaging with.

Alongside these two key individuals, Dr. Wynand de Kock, who first encouraged me to embrace the world of practical theology, has walked alongside me for over a decade. Working with him on Open Seminary has given me the insight I needed to see practical theology worked out in the real world.

In the later stages of this book Sue Jones has been incredibly generous in formatting the material in its final stages. To her I am enormously grateful.

And finally to my lovely wife, Tigs. The lifetime and growth of this book has taken place at the same time as some huge challenges for us as a family. You remain more important than any book, any job, and anything.

ONE

Introduction

PRACTICAL THEOLOGY IN THE REAL WORLD

The world is changing, and changing to such an extent that we can hardly define our problems, let alone attempt to solve them. Perhaps one might counter that the world has always been changing and, in some sense, that of course is true. Change is always knocking on our door, attempting to dismantle and rearrange us. We do not need sociologists and anthropologists to tell us that our world is in a state of intense insecurity, complexity, and inequality. Or, perhaps we do. Perhaps we need the harsh realities of our world to be spelled out again and again until it sinks in and leads to some form of action. Or can this just lead to escapism or denial as one becomes numb to the world around us and our issues?

We live in an uncertain and shifting world. Manuel Castells, in his three-volume series, *The Information Age: Economy, Society and Culture*, is one such attempt to describe this complex world—one that he defines as the network society, a world where many suffer from an acute identity crisis. The following quote from Castells helps to put into more concrete focus what I believe is taking shape:

> This is indeed a time of change, regardless of how we time it. In the last quarter of the twentieth century, a technological revolution, centerd around information, transformed the way we think, we produce, we consume, we trade, we manage, we communicate, we live, we die, we make war, and we make love. A dynamic, global

economy has been constituted around the planet, linking up valuable people and activities from all over the world, while switching off from the networks of power and wealth, people and territories dubbed as irrelevant from the perspective of the dominant interests.[1]

This globalized world that Castells describes is also one of increasing unity, which the historian J. M. Roberts calls a "creeping unity"[2] that finds its most visible expression in modernity. This unity is not so much political, but rather revolves around economics as nations push to modernize. Despite the apparent cultural diversity, it appears that many, if not all, are battling with, or are moving towards, an increasingly modernized world.

Alongside modernism and, in some ways, in opposition to it, is the effect of postmodernism. Although highly debated at present, it still appears that postmodernism is a very real dimension of our world, specifically with regard to the question of epistemology. Some see postmodernism as a subspecies of globalization—both of which in many ways are antithetical to modernism[3]. We shall explore Richard Osmer and Friedrich Schweitzer's definition at a later point when we engage in a more detailed assessment of foundationalism.[4]

---

1. Castells, *The Information Age*, 1.
2. Roberts, *The New Penguin History*, 1174.
3. Osmer and Schweitzer, *Religious Education*, 31.
4. Although foundationalism will be explored later it is important to bring clarity to how this term is distinguished from anti, non and post foundationalism, as many scholars use the terms differently and interchangeably. It is also important to show the relationship between postmodernism and foundationalism. Antifoundationalism (Baronov, *Conceptual Foundations*, 139–40) is the critique of foundationalist assumptions connected with modernism, that like some aspects of postmodernism, leans towards a relativistic outlook. Nonfoundationalism (Thiel, *Nonfoundationalism*, 2) is also a critique of foundationalist modernist assumptions, yet is not relativistic as much as it is a statement of what is "not philosophically tenable." Postfoundationalism accepts many of the criticisms of anti and nonfoundationalism, but seeks to move "creatively" forward to some form of resolution of these philosophical dilemma's (van Huyssteen, *Essays in Postfoundationalist Theology*, 4). Postmodernism is not dissimilar to the various categories of foundationalism just mentioned. It can lean towards a relativistic outlook or have more positive and constructive overtones. Postfoundationalism, with its history in the pragmatic philosophers of the late nineteenth and early twentieth centuries, predates postmodernism (Thiel, *Nonfoundationalism*, 6–7). They are however linked by their critique of modern enlightenment foundationalism and its quest for "unimpeachable foundations of knowledge" (Schrag *The Resources of Rationality*, 23). Chapter two will be a detailed exploration of the similarities and distinctive of foundationalism and postmodernism.

Introduction

It is within this very real changing world, which Castells describes, that I and others seek to practice our theology and to teach others how not to just *learn* theology, but to *do* theology.[5] Or, more specifically, I ask myself whether the theological work in which I engage is simply an exercise in mental trivia and self-gratification, or whether it has anything to offer this world. Has it relevance to real life and "the messy realm of work, love, celebration, and suffering where human beings dwell and thus where Christian life and ministry take place"?[6] Of course, this is the question practical theology as a discipline needs to reflect upon, specifically with regard to methodological questions. Is it relevant to its context and the given historical situation in which it finds itself?

If it is true, as Osmer and Schweitzer argue, that religious education needs to be seen in its interdependent relationship to its given social context,[7] then the task of practical theology is to understand that context and certain aspects of it.[8] A postfoundationalist approach to practical theology would be just one such way of taking one's social context seriously. If we live in a world that is in some way moving beyond modernism, then we need to ask ourselves seriously whether practical theology and theological reflection has moved beyond modernism in its methodological assumptions and understanding of itself. I believe it has and that a postfoundationalist approach can help sharpen that approach even further.

Grenz and Franke argue that the epistemological center of modernism is foundationalism.[9] If they are correct, then a postfoundationalist practical theology becomes exceedingly critical in a globalized and postmodern world. We cannot ignore these realities, for as Ganzevoort fears "we may be outdistanced by the rapid changes in western society and in the people living in it. Where the church is only just catching up with modern man, humankind is already beyond modernism and plunging into a postmodern era."[10]

Moreover, if foundationalism is the epistemological center of modernism, it will, at times, require an evaluation of what the epistemology has spawned so to speak with regard to modernism—its effects. This could be

5. De Gruchy, "Nature, Necessity," 2.
6. Bass, *Practicing Theology*, 1.
7. Osmer and Schweitzer, *Religious Education*, 3.
8. Osmer, *Practical Theology*.
9. Grenz and Franke, *Beyond Foundationalism*, 29–32.
10. Ganzevoort, "The Splintered Cross," 3.

one of the ways then to evaluate a postfoundationalist approach, by examining its effects and results.

Postmodernism, whether heightened modernism or something entirely new, has certainly been a necessary and decisive counterstrike to modernism. It has sought to show the weakness and frailties of modernistic assumptions. Unfortunately, sometimes its proposals have been overtly negative and nihilistic. Müller[11] believes a postfoundationalist perspective allows one to position oneself between these extremes and avoid the tendencies towards relativism and antifoundationalism to which postmodernism drifts.[12] Part of my evaluation of foundationalism would then have to examine what role rationality might have for a postfoundationalist perspective for practical theology, and whether this "chastened rationality" is being affirmed or denied. Here, it is critical that rationality is explored within a postfoundationalist approach to practical theology, as van Huyssteen argues:

> In theology we seek as secure a knowledge as we can achieve, a knowledge that will allow us to understand and where possible to construct theories as better explanations. This goal of theology not only determines the rationality of theology, but very much depends on the way we deal with the problem of justification of cognitive claims in theology. If in both theology and science we want to understand and explain, then the rationality of science is directly relevant to that of theology.[13]

Osmer argues, based on van Huyssteen's understanding of transversal rationality, that cross-disciplinary dialogue, where areas of intersection and divergence are important, will be crucial to this rationality.[14] Müller, in discussing the importance of interdisciplinary engagement for practical theology, states that a postfoundationalist perspective is one that is well suited to this cross-disciplinary dialogue.[15] A postfoundationalist rationality is one that rejects both the *universal rationality* of foundationalism and

---

11. Julian Müller is the first practical theologian that I am aware of who has begun to seriously ask how postfoundationalism can be used in practical theology. Alongside Müller, Osmer has also worked with postfoundationalism. Specifically in the use of a transversal approach and the use of critical realism. Both have been influenced directly with their engagement with Van Huyysteen.

12. Müller, "Post-foundationalist," 1.

13. van Huyssteen, *Essays in Postfoundationalist Theology*, 165.

14. Osmer, *Practical Theology*, 170–72.

15. Müller, "Holistic Pastoral Ministry," 5–6.

Introduction

a *multiversal rationality* of antifoundationalism. By asking these questions with regard to practical theology, the enormity of the task was realized. Once there was a time in history when individuals were able to master most of the known knowledge of a wide variety of disciplines and sciences. Paul Johnson notes that many of the founding fathers of America were politicians, scientists, architects, theologians and philosophers, all rolled into one.[16] Benjamin Franklin was a member of twenty-eight different academies and learned societies. Those times are surely past. Today we have sub-disciplines within disciplines due to the overwhelming amount of knowledge and information with which one must interact—certainly part of the effects of modernism. Even within sub-disciplines, it becomes hard for but a few to be able to master the totality of their discipline. Practical theology must certainly suffer from this problem. The vast amount of information, books, seminars, journals, and organizations must result in a situation where all but a few are aware of the many developments and perspectives within this discipline. Ganzevoort laments at times the lack of a common object, method, and aim which places practical theology as a discipline at risk.[17] The fact that, in many ways, practical theology relies on other theological disciplines, as well as other empirical sciences, only compounds the problem. Moore reminds us of this breadth within the discipline and notes: "Something of the confusion within practical theology, as well as the creativity and wide compass. Unlike scholars in some religious and theological disciplines, practical theologians (taken as a whole) do not have to challenge themselves to broaden their scope, sources, and their methods."[18]

I'm not sure I can claim to have mastered the field and practice of practical theology, a discipline inherently difficult to describe.[19] The choice of material has been driven by my own encounters with other practical theologians and their recommended works. I am also influenced in my selection by my own temperament, theological history, church history, gender, and societal and economic makeup (to mention but a few). My contribution to this field is in bringing various concepts and materials, with

---

16. Johnson, *A History of the American People*, 139.
17. Ganzevoort, "Forks in the Road."
18. Moore, "Editorial Practical Theology," 163–67.
19. Veiling, *Practical Theology*, 3.

my experience to a description of a postfoundationalist approach to practical theology.[20]

It is part of my own local and contextual battle, my own pastoral concerns and vocational experiences that has led me to this work. It is because of this that I began to explore the questions of foundationalism and its implications for practical theology. The importance of this and understanding my "backstory" leads me directly to some personal confessions.

CONFESSIONS OF A FOUNDATIONALIST EVANGELICAL

To many this might seem a strange point to take a personal excursion of this sort. It will be argued that it is important as it gives context to much of what follows and the positions taken, or not taken. It is also important in that it is Grenz's proposal that theology, and specifically evangelical theology, must take into account the move beyond foundationlism on which so much of its deliberations are built. And the evangelical community is the one from which I have grown.

John De Gruchy wrote a book entitled *Being Human: Confessions of a Christian Humanist*. In many ways, I would perhaps be moving towards defining myself as such. However, there is something about the term "evangelical" for which an affinity is felt, if not only for emotional and historical reasons. Defining terms is notoriously a sticky business, as De Gruchy notes: "Terms like liberal and conservative, fundamentalist and evangelical, religious and secular, creation and evolution, humanist and even Christian, are laden with diverse meanings as a result of different cultural experiences."[21]

Roger Olson, like De Gruchy, notes that the word "evangelical" can mean just such vastly different things.[22] In Europe, the word "evangelical" refers essentially to Protestantism. It is a form of Christianity that is neither Eastern Orthodox nor Roman Catholic, and stands in the tradition of Luther, Calvin, and Cranmer. In the United Kingdom, "evangelical" is often used to refer to the revivalist movements of Wesley and Whitefield. In America, it is generally a form of Protestant Christianity that is "conserva-

---

20. Understanding the importance of how one's personal background impacts one's research and how the researcher is considered a given in theological circles. This is spelled out in virtually any recent methodology textbook. There simply is no neutral research that can claim complete objectivity and pretend to dispel any form of subjectivity.

21. De Gruchy, *Being Human*, 4.

22. Olson, *The Mosaic of Christian Belief*, 13.

tive in theology, conversionist and evangelistic, Biblicist, and is focused on Jesus Christ."[23] It crosses various denominations and places a high emphasis on a personal relationship with Jesus. Stanley Grenz widens this slightly by understanding the root word of evangelical in the Greek as "good news": "Understood in terms of commitment to the gospel, evangelical would—or should—characterize every segment of the church and every Christian, regardless of theological loyalties, background or experiences."[24]

Grenz believes that, at its heart, evangelicalism is a way of being Christian where experiencing God is central.[25] It is a commitment to understand this experience of God primarily through the Scriptures as its starting point. Of course, how one comes to understand the word "gospel" has radical implications for how one lives out one's faith in the world.

I was "converted" to the Christian faith at the early age of eleven years and remember the day clearly as I was asked to raise my hand in a small congregational church hall with nine others. I cannot remember exactly what was said, but remember that I needed my sins forgiven, and that Jesus had done this for me on the cross. This experience was common for many within the evangelical tradition, as well as those from other traditions. De Gruchy speaks of his own experience of conversion in his teens, when he made a "commitment to Jesus Christ as saviour and Lord"[26] and how that decision affected the rest of his life. It was the same for me.

However, what happened next put me within a certain stream of the evangelical movement. I was asked if I wanted to be baptized in the Holy Spirit and receive the gift of tongues. I consented and was baptized thus, but now no longer know if I even agree with the terminology and confess a deep suspicion with much that happens within the charismatic and Pentecostal movements. Something did happen to me though, and I experienced God. Before long, I went to the Congregational church on a Sunday morning, a Pentecostal mega-church in the afternoon, and church again in the evening; it consumed my life.

In high school, I moved away from the faith after a friend's brother died and I could not figure out why my prayers for healing were not answered. I had thought that I simply needed to "name it and claim it." After a foray into drugs, alcohol, and generally unwholesome behavior, I returned

---

23. Ibid.
24. Grenz, *Revisioning Evangelical Theology*, 22.
25. Ibid., 34.
26. De Gruchy, *Being Human*, 13.

to faith in my final year of high school —to the shock and amazement of many of my peers. From the time of my conversion, I knew that I wanted to be a minister, but fluctuated in my early years between the desire to be an evangelist, pastor, teacher, and prophet. When told I could be all four by being an apostle, the option was obvious!

At this point, I began attending a Bible school in the evenings, completing two years. A year after school, I began a course in intellectual and social history at the Pentecostal mega-church of which I was a part. I remember buying Francis Schaeffer's complete works and devouring almost every book.

During that year, I was told why every other belief system was faulty and how to decipher that philosophically, and was told what the "biblical Christian worldview" was, and how that could be implemented in every area of life. This would be the same from New York to New Delhi. In reflection on this time, despite total commitment to the ideology, experientially I was never quite sure; I always wanted to push certain boundaries in the opposite direction. Despite this, I would spend Friday nights praying through the night, committed to revival in South Africa, and reading every book on the topic I could find. It was in this matrix of educational and experiential realities by which my Christian faith and outlook essentially took on a modernistic foundationalist perspective, based on Scripture as an inerrant encyclopaedia of knowledge to be applied to any context. Grenz argues that both liberals and conservatives fall under the spell of the foundationalist agenda—the conservatives using the Bible as their foundation, and liberals, religious experience.[27] I had fallen on the conservative side.

Later, I began studies at a local South African university through correspondence. It was a journey that would change my life. I remember the experience of reading a book by Hans Küng, *Credo: The Apostles' Creed Explained for Today* and, being disgusted with what Küng says, threw the book across the room. I desperately tried to figure out where he was wrong. (Subsequently, Küng has become one of my favorite theologians.) I remember also being exposed to Barth and Pannenberg and being intrigued and inspired.

Until six years ago, I remained part of what was essentially a charismatic church, yet vastly more moderate than the Pentecostal church of which I had previously been part. Despite this, their views were by no means vastly different. However, the Pentecostal church was committed to

---

27. Grenz, *Renewing the Center*, 189.

changing society through biblical ideology by taking over the centers of power, while the charismatic church by converting the masses. However, they were both committed to biblical inerrancy and doctrinal purity. I was still within a predominantly modernist and foundationalist institution. While studying, and at the same time being involved in all these different churches, an unbelievable dissonance was created for me. Things came to a head when my views on the role of women conflicted with their more traditional view.

So where am I now? I am no longer committed to biblical inerrancy, but consider the Bible my first port of call, and a reasonably reliable account of the life of Jesus. It is the *critical realist* understanding of the text to which I adhere, an approach that I believe to be postfoundationalist, which will be engaged with in more detail at a later stage. This will also become immensely important when examining the role of the Bible as a source for practical theology. I agree with van Huyssteen's statement: "Personally I am convinced that no theologian who is trying to determine what the authority of the Bible might mean for today, and to identify the epistemological status of the Bible in theological reflection, can avoid the important issues raised by some qualified form of critical realism for theology."[28]

My critical realist and nonfoundationalist reading of the Bible has also led me to affirm that the gospel is equated not just with the salvation of souls, but is far broader than that. Catholics are not the whores of Babylon, but partners and friends. Islam is not a demonic religion, but one which should be engaged with mutual dialogue and respect. Am I still evangelical? Perhaps not. However, I still value the Bible; I still believe individuals' lives ought to be changed to conform with God's dream for the world, and I still believe God can be experienced.

My nostalgia for evangelicalism will be evident throughout this work. Many names of theologians will pop up, but will not dominate. A commitment will be found to understand theologians, such as Olson and Grenz, as ones who have attempted to redefine evangelicalism. A desire to interact with McLaren, who has attempted to broaden the evangelical vista from its narrow fundamentalist expressions, will also be found. Yet, my commitment to the broader dimensions of Christianity are now stronger than ever—both liberal and conservative, Protestant or Catholic, first or third world, mainstream or free church.

---

28. van Huyssteen, *Essays in Postfoundationalist Theology*, 129.

Postfoundationalist Reflections in Practical Theology

My personal journey as a theologian, with all its high points and low points, doubts and fears, is perhaps best described by Paul Tillich in the following quote:

> There are many amongst us who believe within themselves that they can never become good theologians, that they could do better in almost any other realm. Yet they cannot imagine that their existence could be anything other than theological existence. Even if they had to give up theology as their vocational work, they would never cease to ask the theological question. It would pursue them into every realm. They would be bound to it, actually, if not vocationally. They could not be sure that they could fulfil its demands, but they would be sure they were in its bondage. They would believe those things in their hearts belong to the assembly of God. They are grasped by the divine spirit. They have received the gift of knowledge. They are theologians.[29]

I resonate with Tillich's description here, which demonstrates the personal nature of doing theology and the reason for this attempt to share this theological journey to the present. I have also shared my personal faith narrative because I think it illustrates, in many ways, the challenge of doing practical theology. My Christian history is heavily loaded with modernistic assumptions, expressed through concepts, such as biblical inerrancy.

Evangelicals are also not noted for their desire to reflect on their assumptions and methodological commitments.[30] I now believe it critical that any conscious Christian and theologian ought to reflect on their methodological foundations.[31] It was through a process of having my epistemological roots exposed that led to a collapse of faith and an embracing of postmodern beliefs and ideas. In many ways, my present journey has allowed me to settle down somewhere in the middle, a critical realism beyond foundationalism.

THE STRUCTURE OF THIS WORK

The very personal story and battle with foundationalism discussed above is really the methodological starting point for this journey. It is part of my own local and contextual battle, my pastoral concern and vocational

---

29. Tillich, *The Shaking of the Foundations*, 125.
30. McGrath, "Evangelical Theological Method," 16.
31. Stone and Duke, *How to Think Theologically*, 60.

experience. It is from this base that I began to explore the questions of foundationalism and its implications for practical theology. This led me to a broad-based review of practical theology against the background of the epistemological and philosophical discussions of foundationalism and postfoundationalism. In my doctoral dissertation I argued that in many ways practical theology has indeed moved beyond foundationalism, and I will make the same argument here. But further than that I will attempt to focus more intentionally on the specific shape and form a postfoundationalist approach may offer practical theology as a discipline.

In the journey to be embarked upon, the following areas must be discussed and engaged with. I will begin by exploring what foundationalism actually is, and how it relates to both postmodernism and modernism. This will also involve understanding critical realism as potentially one way toward a postfoundationalist perspective.

Chapter 3 will attempt to examine broadly some issues regarding practical theology as a discipline. This will be done initially by defining terminology. Having defined the terminology, the historical development of practical theology will be considered. Aside from again helping us to understand the present state of practical theology, it will also highlight the paradigm shift that has taken place in the discipline, and help us to gain a clearer understanding of whether a move beyond foundationalism has indeed taken place.

This brief historical survey is being conducted for the reasons mentioned earlier, and should be evaluated as such—has practical theology moved beyond the foundationalist assumptions? In what ways can a deeper embrace of a postfoundationalist perspective aid practical theology in its endeavors?

Having at this point done a detailed engagement with the idea of foundationalism and its consequences, as well as a brief appraisal of the history of practical theology, an attempt will be made to delineate if, and how, practical theology has moved beyond foundationalism. Without pre-empting the discussion, I will argue that a return to context and the pastoral cycle appears to move in this direction. A re-evaluation of the sources for practical theology would seem to be moving in this way too—both in widening the sources as an example, but also in a re-evaluation of the epistemological foundations of those sources. This will involve a detailed discussion of the correlational hermeneutic. Further to that, the question of application will be explored as the full turn of the pastoral cycle. In all of this I hope to make some specific comments and suggestions as to how practical theology can continue to move beyond foundationalism, and what shape that might begin to take.

TWO

Foundationalism Explored

Twentieth-century thought has increasingly had to reckon with the judgements and claims of an approach to philosophical criticism called *nonfoundationalism*. No particular philosopher can be named the founder of this critical approach, nor does a school of thinkers faithful to the tenets of nonfoundationalism exist. At most, one can speak of a commitment to a style of philosophizing shared by a number of thinkers, often in very different ways.[1]

The earlier reference to John Thiel illustrates just how difficult the task to understand foundationalism might be. A brief clarification of terminology might prove helpful prior to our detailed discussion. F. Leron Schults sees nonfoundationalism as essentially a relativistic position, rejecting foundationalism and the certainty it claims and professes.[2] Thiel[3] simply states that nonfoundationalism is rejecting what is not philosphically tenable.[4] Although Schults sees nonfoundationalism and antifoundationalism as the same, I think this needs further nuance. The social scientist David Baranov argues that antifoundationalism is in some ways seen as a "destruction of everything."[5] Postfoundationalism then is the desire to steer a middle ground between the relativism of nonfoundationalism and anti-

---

1. Thiel, *Nonfoundationalism*, 1.
2. Schults, *The Postfoundationalist Task*, 31.
3. Thiel, *Nonfoundationalism*, 2.
4. For a good critique of Thiel's nonfoundationalism see Schults, *The Postfoundationalist Task*, 36–38. Here Schults argued that Thiel cannot see further than the two options of nonfoundationalism or foundationalism.
5. Baronov, *The Conceptual Foundations*, 139.

foundationalism and the certainty of foundationalism. Schults describes it thus, "Postfoundationalism aims to develop a plausible model of theological rationality that charts a course (to switch metaphors) between the Scylla of foundationalist dogmatism and the Charybdis of nonfoundationalist relativism.[6]" When introducing critical realism later as an important aspect of postfoundationalism the work of Wentzel van Huyssteen and Roy Bhaskar will become crucial. Bhaskar particularly focuses on critical realism as a way of viewing reality and knowledge that enables us to also avoid the pitfalls of relativism and certainty. Andrew Collier, in his analysis of Bhaskar uses the same analogy as Schults, where Bhaskar sails between "Scylla and Charybdis, irrationalism and a narrowly calculated rationalism."[7] In other words, critical realism sails between naïve realism and relativism.

An overzealous focus on postmodernism has perhaps clouded the issues involved. An often uncritical embrace of postmodernism or, at its opposite extreme, an uncritical rejection of it, causes furious debate in the quest for epistemological primacy. Müller cautions us against both extremes, but still warns of the serious threat of relativism and antifoundationalist theories, "which are a real threat to practical theology."[8] Even if the focus has revolved around postmodernism, perhaps due to the popularity of its proponents that more resemble a school, is there a possibility that understanding postmodernism might actually enlighten our perspectives regarding a postfoundationalist theology? What is the link between a postfoundational theology and postmodernism? Van Huyssteen recognizes that any discussion of foundationalism must be confronted with an understanding of postmodernism: "The either/or of foundationalism versus nonfoundationalism, reveals that here we not only are dealing with modernity's challenge to theological reflection, but have in fact already moved into the far more complex challenge of contemporary postmodern thought.[9]" Therefore, we need to understand the challenge of postmodernism and how it relates to post foundationlist thinking.

---

6. Schults, *The Postfoundationalist Task*, 36.
7. Collier, *Critical Realism*, x.
8. Müller, "Post-foundationalist," 1.
9. van Huyssteen, *Essays in Postfoundationalist Theology*, 74.

THE CHALLENGE OF POSTMODERNISM

"The Challenge of Postmodernism" is borrowed from a chapter in a book by Schrag entitled, *The Resources of Rationality: A Response to the Postmodern Challenge*. A quote from that chapter might be a good entry point to our discussion, as Schrag notes the difficulty when engaging with the topic:

> Anyone attempting to provide a sketch of postmodernism has to contend with a somewhat curious diversity of portraits on display both in the academy and on the wider cultural scene. This diversity is in part the result of grammatical variations in the identification of the phenomenon at issue. In the proliferating discussions of the topic the vocabulary often shifts from "the postmodern" to "postmodernity" to "postmodernism" without clear indications of what, if anything, is at stake in such shifts.[10]

Schrag, certainly, is right in his assessment of the linguistic labyrinth that is postmodernism. There is very little agreement on exactly its nature and scope. At the same time, it has crept into our popular imagination, and even our church circles, with a wide variety and diversity of opinion on what it actually is. It is often a heated topic, as McLaren recently noted in an essay entitled, "Church Emerging: Or Why I Still use the Term *Postmodern* but with Mixed Feelings."

As mentioned earlier on in this book, the terms "postmodernism" and its partner "postmodernity" are still highly debated topics. Some see it as an all-pervasive reality that has consumed the Western world. Others see it as a reactionary movement that is a small component (or shadow) of the larger march of modernism. Further still, many see it as one aspect of globalization where "it is a configuration of cultural elements that represents one and only one way of responding to the globalization of culture."[11]

I, for one, believe postmodernism is more pervasive at the level of everyday culture than some would allow for. Ganzevoort makes this argument and believes postmodernism is an attitude "of individuals and groups that is becoming wide spread in our time."[12] I also believe our world is a mix of both pre-modern, modern, and postmodern realities and that there is a general consensus that postmodernism has certainly played a significant part in raising the right questions with regard to knowledge and rationality.

---

10. Schrag, *The Resources of Rationality*, 13.
11. Osmer and Schweitzer, *Religious Education*, 66.
12. Ganzevoort, "The Splintered Cross," 46.

However, I agree with Schrag that it is "rationality, and particularly rationality as it figures in the philosophical discourse of modernity, that has been challenged by postmodernism."[13]

Schrag goes on to say that the varied voices of postmodernism really all attempt to critique the overreliance on reason, and "specifically as this over determination was played out in the modern epistemological paradigm."[14] As van Huyssteen argues, postmodernism is a rejection of all forms of epistemological foundationalism of this modern paradigm.[15]

This, of course, is the direct relevance and importance of clarifying and establishing postmodernism and its relationship to foundationalism, and therefore asking the broader questions of whether practical theology has indeed moved beyond foundationalism and indeed how it can be enhanced with postfoundationalist perspectives.

Though, before entering into a detailed discussion around foundationalism, a brief sketch of the main contours of postmodern thought would be helpful. I am interested in the philosophical and epistemological consequences of postmodernism and its effects for practical theology and foundationalism. These concerns will guide this historical sketch.

What Is Postmodernism?

The modern world was characterized by the affirmation that knowledge is objective, certain, and good[16] and symbolized by a positive attitude towards the future "nurtured by a profound faith in the resources of science and technology to deliver us from social ills."[17]

There was a claim to view the world objectively and to place knowledge on a firm foundation. In his popular novel, *A New Kind of Christian*, Brian McLaren's fictional character, Neo, describes modernism well: "It was an age aspiring to absolute certainty, which we believed, would yield absolute certainty and knowledge. In modernity, the ultimate intelligibility of the universe was assumed. What was still unknown was ultimately knowable. Also assumed was the highest faith in human reason."[18]

13. Schrag, *The Resources of Rationality*, 7.
14. Ibid.
15. van Huyssteen, *Essays in Postfoundationalist Theology*, 2.
16. Grenz, *A Primer on Postmodernism*, 4.
17. Schrag, *The Resources of Rationality*, 43.
18. McLaren, *A New Kind of Christian*, 17.

Foundationalism Explored

The shift away from the assumptions and presuppositions of modernity can be seen in the postmodern philosophers, Derrida, Foucault, and Rorty. Based on deconstruction, these philosophers argue that one cannot grasp a unified objective picture of the world. All we are left with are differing perspectives on the same reality. Truth is not absolute, but relative to the community in which we find ourselves.[19] Most will reject my gross oversimplification of Derrida, Foucault, and Rorty. Schrag has warned of the dangers of trying to bundle such diverse individuals together and attempting to see their common threads, seeing it as akin to trying to pin down a droplet of mercury. Despite this, I think Schrag is correct in asserting that their commonality becomes apparent in their challenge to the rationality of modernity and the "overdetermination of reason, and specifically as this overestimation was played out in the modern epistemological paradigm."[20]

This reaction was against a modernism that has its roots in Rene Descartes (1596–1650) who was viewed as the first "great rationalist philosopher,"[21] the first outstanding thinker of modern times,[22] and who was also labeled "the father of modern philosophy."[23] Descartes sought to ground belief in some form of rational certitude in mathematics with "foundations rationally established by intuition or deduction."[24] Grenz summarizes Descartes aptly: "Descartes's intent was to devise a method of investigation that could facilitate the discovery of those truths that were absolutely certain. . . . In establishing the centrality of the human mind in this manner, Descartes set the agenda for philosophy for the next three hundred years."[25]

Now, of course, it was not Descartes alone who was responsible for the modern project in all of its forms. Tolstoy is always quick to remind us of the "swarm" of history, and that great individuals are rather products of history before producers.[26] Even in Descartes's lifetime, those like Pascal had perceived the whole "relativity of purely rational, mathematical certainty."[27]

19. Grenz, *A Primer on Postmodernism*, 7–8.
20. Schrag, *The Resources of Rationality*, 7.
21. Raeper and Smith, *A Brief Guide to Ideas*, 42.
22. Küng, *Does God Exist?*, 5.
23. Grenz, *A Primer on Postmodernism*, 63.
24. Küng, *Does God Exist?*, 18.
25. Grenz, *A Primer on Postmodernism*, 64.
26. Tolstoy, *War and Peace*, 657.
27. Küng, *Does God Exist?*, 50.

Postfoundationalist Reflections in Practical Theology

John Locke (1632–1704) did not depart much from Descartes's quest for certain knowledge based on foundations. Murphy argues the same with regard to Hume, despite his attack on Cartesian foundationalism.[28] Locke though, instead of a rationalist approach, was formed in an empirical approach that sought to ground knowledge in experience, where mind is a blank sheet written on by what comes through our senses.[29] Both Descartes and Locke will be crucial in our link between postmodernism and foundationalism.

Immanuel Kant was also one who questioned many of the assumptions that emerged during the Enlightenment that had flowed from Descartes and others. However, despite this, those like Grenz believe that "his key reformulation of the ideals of the age of reason breathed new life into the Enlightenment project and gave it the shape it would take in the modern era."[30] For Kant: "Knowledge begins with experience, it does not arise from experience. Knowledge has its genuine origin in the forms of intuition, the schema of the imagination, and the categories of the understanding, that reside *a priori* in the human mind."[31] Kant believed that the content of these experiences were not, according to Collier, "the world in itself" but "rather imposed this knowable form on it."[32]

So, how did this modern epistemological project begin to slowly unravel? Most will point to Friedrich Nietzsche (1844–1900) as the one who led the way.[33] He was indeed one of the formative reasons for the breakup.[34] He attacked Kant and others whose quest was for true beliefs.[35] He was, without doubt, a foe of modernity:

> Before he died though, Nietzsche formulated most of the themes that would be essential to the development of the postmodern intellectual climate. Above all, he established the course towards postmodernism with his thoroughgoing rejection of Enlightenment principles. . . . lying at the foundation of Nietzsche's attack

---

28. Murphy, *Beyond Liberalism*, 86.
29. Raeper and Smith. *A Brief Guide to Ideas*, 90; Thiel, *Nonfoundationalism*, 5.
30. Grenz, *A Primer on Postmodernism*, 74.
31. Schrag, *The Resources of Rationality*, 2.
32. Collier, *Critical Realism*, 21.
33. Murphy, *Beyond Liberalism*, 87.
34. Schrag, *The Resources of Rationality*, 43–44.
35. Raeper and Smith, *A Brief Guide to Ideas*, 168.

on modernism is his rejection of the Enlightenment concept of truth.[36]

Following after Nietzsche, a host of philosophers came who sought to challenge the modern epistemological project. One can quickly devise a "canon of postmodern thinkers which would likely include the works of Derrida, Lyotard, Deleuze, Guattari, Bastaille, Foucault, Baudrillard, Rorty, Feyerabend—and surely Nietzsche and Heidegger."[37]

The postmodern philosophers sought to attack the quest for universal meaning and truth that the modern philosophers, from Descartes through to Immanual Kant, had sought. The Enlightenment project for progress in society, based on beliefs that are certain, now begins to unravel. Most notably with Nietzsche, and then with the postmodern philosophers mentioned in Schrag's canon. Now, knowledge is fragmented, indeterminate and non-universal.[38] Ganzevoort picks up on this fragmented aspect of knowledge and notes that it is one of the defining aspects highlighting the shift from modern to postmodern:

> What is it that makes postmodernism so radical and critical? In my view the core threat and challenge lies in the fact that postmodern thinking is going beyond rationalism, because it takes it's starting point in the fragmentation of life. Whereas for modern man fragmentation is a consequence (and often regarded as a negative one) of modernism, for postmodern man there is nothing but fragmentation.[39]

The claims of rationality are now problematized.[40] Van Gelder perhaps best articulates the postmodern condition as follows:

> Describing the postmodern condition and attempting to theorize about it are producing a new vocabulary that can sound strange at first. Concepts such as indeterminacy, deconstruction, diversity, decentering, and the aestheticization of all of life challenge the vocabulary of modernity, which emphasized prediction, certainty, absolutes, centers, and the privileging of a particular style as a preferred culture.[41]

36. Grenz, *A Primer on Postmodernism*, 88.
37. Schrag, *The Resources of Rationality*, 6.
38. van Huyssteen, *Essays in Postfoundationalist Theology*, 75.
39. Ganzevoort, "The Splintered Cross," 48.
40. Schrag, *The Resources of Rationality*, 7.
41. Van Gelder, "Mission in the Emerging Post Modern Condition," 114.

Postmodernism has been taken in a host of different directions by various people. One of the expressions of postmodernism has been that of *positive postmodernism*. Van Gelder explains its approach to truth as follows:

> It is their belief that the fact that truth is relative does not rob it of all meaning. The worlds in which we live, both physical and social, are real and we can come to know meaningful things about them. They simply caution that we can't possess knowledge about them in an absolute sense. We have to use adjectives such as contextual, perspectival and interpreted to define both the process by which we come to know and the content that we learn.[42]

The postmodern turn that we have been discussing has resulted in what some define as a *chastened rationality*. Franke believes that postmodernism, with its resulting chastened rationality, leads to a rejection of the epistemological certainty to which foundationalism adheres.[43] This epistemological shift leads to a contextual epistemology and one that is nonfoundational. But, what exactly is foundationalism then?

FOUNDATIONALISM

Here, a brief moment has been spent traversing the historical journey of postmodernism, which I believe is directly relevant to the discussion regarding foundationalism. I offer an extended quote from van Huyssteen that he believes best illustrates this link, while at the same time providing a basic definition of foundationalism:

> Postmodernism is, as I see it, first of all a very pointed rejection of all forms of epistemological foundationalism, as well as of its ubiquitous, accompanying metanarratives that so readily claim to legitimize all our knowledge, judgements, decisions and actions. Foundationalism, as is generally defined today, is the thesis that all our beliefs can be justified by appealing to some item of knowledge that is self-evident or indubitable. Foundationalism in this epistemological sense therefore always implies the holding of a position of inflexibility and infallibility, because in the process of justifying our knowledge claims, we are able to invoke ultimate

---

42. Ibid., 134.
43. Franke, *The Character of Theology*, 26.

foundations on which we construct the evidential support systems of our various convictional beliefs.⁴⁴

In many ways, we are all foundationalists in our attempt to root our knowledge in something more basic or on various other presuppositions. Grenz and Franke note: "In its broadest sense, foundationalism is merely the acknowledgment of the seemingly obvious observation that not all beliefs we hold (or assertions we formulate) are on the same level, but that some beliefs (or assertions) anchor others. Stated on the opposite manner, certain of our beliefs (or assertions) receive their support from other beliefs (or assertions) that are more 'basic' or 'foundational.'"⁴⁵

However, the foundationalist agenda goes further than this and hopes to ground our knowing on a basis that can provide us with certainty and deliver us from error. This basis is regarded as universal and context free and is available to any rational person.⁴⁶ This approach can be either deductive or inductive, from innate ideas or the sensory world.

Rene Descartes is viewed by many as the father of foundationalism in his attempt to establish a sure foundation for knowledge in that he:

> claimed to have established the foundations of knowledge by appeal to the mind's own experience of certainty. On this basis he began to construct anew the human knowledge edifice. Descartes was convinced that this epistemological program yields knowledge that is certain, culture—and tradition—free, universal, and reflective of a reality that exists outside the mind (this latter being a central feature of a position known as "metaphysical realism" or simply "realism").⁴⁷

Descartes is central to the story, not only because of his influence, but because nonfoundational critics see his thought as paradigmatic of foundationalism.⁴⁸ Descartes believed knowledge could be free from doubt and error with simple and known truths on which knowledge could be based.⁴⁹

Others, like John Locke (1632–1704), argued that sense experience is the foundation of knowledge, which is also known as empiricism.⁵⁰ Hume

44. van Huyssteen, *Essays in Postfoundationalist Theology*, 2.
45. Grenz and Franke, *Beyond Foundationalism*, 29.
46. Ibid., 30.
47. Ibid.
48. Thiel, *Nonfoundationalism*, 3.
49. Küng, *Does God Exist?*, 7.
50. Grenz and Franke, *Beyond Foundationalism*, 32.

(1711–1776), also part of the British empiricist tradition, "argued that sense experience and not ideas provides a grounding for philosophical inquiry."[51] Kant's challenge to the empiricist tradition was already discussed when he was examined here in relation to postmodernism. He argued for the *a priori* givenness of the ideas in the mind, which are the first foundational principles for philosophy.[52]

In our discussion of postmodernism, we neglected to mention the pragmatic tradition. Indeed, most discussions of postmodernism tend to focus overly on Nietzsche and the French philosophers.[53] Thiel has done outstanding work in tracing the philosophical history of nonfoundationalism, but space does not permit a detailed recounting of that journey. In summary of the pragmatist's contribution, he has the following to say with regard to the early pragmatists, Pierce (1839–1914), James (1842–1910) and Dewey (1859–1952):

> Their common concerns represent the beginning of nonfoundational sensibilities in the modern philosophical tradition. First, the pragmatists all rejected the Cartesian method of establishing the first principles of philosophy as a necessary propaedeutic to philosophical inquiry itself. Second, all rejected the metaphysics of understanding in which either sense experience or ideas were privileged as the authoritative basis for knowing, as the foundations for the truth of the philosophical system. Third, all rejected the traditional rationalist implications of ideas. This contextual and foundationless conception of truth was the most characteristic mark of the philosophies of pragmatism.[54]

The discussion of postmodernism neglected to mention Ludwig Wittgenstein (1889–1951) who followed on from Nietzsche. In his discussion of Wittgenstein, Grenz states that, for him, language has become a social phenomenon, which has its meaning only in relation to that social

---

51. Thiel, *Nonfoundationalism*, 5.

52. Ibid.

53. Nancey Murphy (*Beyond Liberalism*, 87) has also picked up on this. She shifted the historical development of postmodernism from the so-called "continental philosophers" to its earlier history in the Anglo-American tradition. In what is to come I will briefly make mention of Thiel's work (*Nonfoundationalism*) where he surveyed the history of the early Pragmatic philosophers who were challenging foundationalist assumptions. Like Thiel, Murphy also turns to Quine as of the key early developments in postmodernity and the challenge to foundationalist thinking.

54. Thiel, *Nonfoundationalism*, 10.

interaction.⁵⁵ Thiel makes the direct link of Wittgenstein's understanding of language as another nail in the foundationalist coffin as now there are "no first principles on which a context of meaning rests but only the context itself, a network of interrelated and mutually constitutive meanings."[56]

Thiel then leads to a discussion on nonfoundational philosophers, such as Sellars, Quine, and Rorty. Sellars attacks what he calls the "myth of the given."[57] It matters not whether the givenness is based on rationalist or empiricist assumptions: "Givenness becomes problematic when a certain dimension of experience is imbued with authority and regarded as a foundation for the other claims to knowledge in a conceptual scheme."[58]

If Sellars attacks the *myth of the given*, Quine attacks the *myth of the museum*. This is an attempt to distribute its foundationalism into the actual conceptual scheme or theory itself, by which meaning is then passed onto the exhibits within the museum.[59] For Quine, this simply falls prey to the same context-driven nature of language and the "rootedness of language use in sensory experience."[60]

Enter Richard Rorty, who we have already met in our discussion of postmodernism and Schrag's canon of postmodern philosophers. Rorty attempts to show how the whole Western philosophical tradition has sought to distinguish between the mental and physical worlds. Here, an extended quote from Thiel will be offered in order to best explain this assumption that Rorty attacks. These considerations will be vital in our following discussion of critical realism as a way forward.

> Whether rationalists or empiricists configured the mental world, they posited its experience as a grounding for any knowledge that claimed to be genuine. In this noetic schematism, thinking (or experiencing) is regarded as an activity that mirrors reality, presenting its truth immediately and firsthand within its very operations. Whether traditional philosophy portrayed reality and its truth as supersensible ideas, the object of sense impressions, or the thing in itself, its privileging of some dimension of mental life as a direct, epistemic avenue to that reality took shape in the assumption that knowledge must have foundations to support the

---

55. Grenz, *A Primer on Postmodernism*, 114.
56. Thiel, *Nonfoundationalism*, 11.
57. Ibid., 12.
58. Ibid., 13.
59. Ibid., 19.
60. Ibid., 20.

> greater share of epistemic claims incapable themselves of direct immediate validation.[61]

Rorty believes that foundationalism, basically, is the same as forms of religious and political fundamentalisms.[62] Both seek for absolute certainty, attempt to dispel myth, and seek "the promise of ready-made answers."[63]

My earlier foray into philosophical history was an attempt to highlight the foundationalist philosophers and their ideas that promoted a foundationalist understanding of reality and truth. It then moved on briefly to look at those who sought to challenge this foundationalism. Of course, there are a variety of positions amongst the nonfoundationalist philosophers. There are also variations of foundationalism itself, on a scale from soft to strong. However, the desire to ground one's beliefs on a sure foundation is common to all of them.

This foundationalism spawns a realist metaphysic that has a strong preference for a correspondence theory of truth,[64] which, of course, is so much of what the nonfoundational philosophers have attacked. I reject the view—that Thiel might be affirming—that a realist metaphysic naturally and only leads to foundationalism. Grenz and Franke have argued that Wolfart Pannenberg is one who has sought to move beyond the correspondence theory of truth[65] while affirming a realist metaphysic. Pannenberg himself has affirmed his preference to be understood as a postfoundationalist.[66] Thiel is correct to criticize a correspondence theory of truth. This theory basically states that what one says about the world can be accurately portrayed in language. This common-sense approach is called into doubt though by difficulties in the way in which language is seen to accurately

---

61. Ibid., 24.

62. Religious fundamentalism, or Christian fundamentalism, is here seen as basically forms of foundationalism (ibid.). Grenz and Franke, *Beyond Foundationalism*, 37 agree that much of Christian fundamentalism, whether using tradition or Scripture, is simply caught in a foundationalist spell. The foundationalist spell of inherent foundations finds its home in Christian fundamentalisms affirmation of an inerrant bible or inerrant tradition.

63. Thiel, *Nonfoundationalism*, 24.

64. Ibid., 30.

65. Grenz and Franke, *Beyond Foundationalism*, 45 and 43.

66. Pannenberg states of Schults (in the foreword to *The Postfoundationalist Task*): "He is correct in placing me neither in the foundationalist camp nor among certain forms of nonfoundationalism that surrender the rational quest for truth. I feel rather sympathetic with the position he describes as postfoundationalist."

represent reality.⁶⁷ How Wittgenstein dealt with these issues and how Quine's myth of the museum exposed the fallacy of this position have already been discussed. Could it be that critical realism could be a reasonable way forward out of the idealist/naïve realist correspondence theory of truth and meaning? This could become helpful for practical theology in understanding how it engages both its context and sources.

Postmodernism has raised questions as to whether such sure knowledge is possible, let alone desirable.⁶⁸ Franke notes that the questions posed by postmodern philosophy struck at two of the main tenets of foundationalism. It rejected the belief in absolute certainty and universality, which is seen as an impossible dream of finite humans. Secondly, the idea of the inherent goodness of knowledge collapses under the weight of human selfishness and sin and the desire to control and manipulate knowledge at other people's expense.⁶⁹

Thiel is forthright in his conclusion regarding foundationalism and its demise on the philosophical landscape: "That nonfoundational criticism is now practiced by a majority of contemporary philosophers testifies to the cogency of its analysis, the adequacy of its explanation, and its consistency with experience."⁷⁰ If a foundationalist correspondence theory of truth and knowledge is truly dead with its realist and idealist assumptions, what could be our way forward?

POSTFOUNDATIONALISM

To state the obvious from our previous discussion—postfoundationalism is the move beyond the absolute certainties touted by modernism and foundationalist philosophies based on a naïve realist metaphysic. It also seeks to avoid the other danger of relativism and certain forms of postmodernism. Most notable here is the work of Wentzel van Huyssteen from Princeton Theological Seminary. Schults believes he most clearly describes the way forward, or the *middle way* as a "third epistemological and hermeneutical option that avoids the extremes of both dogmatic foundationalism and relativistic nonfoundationalism."⁷¹ Julian Müller, influenced by his engage-

---

67. Cartledge, *Practical Theology*, 42–43.
68. Franke, *The Character of Theology*, 27.
69. Ibid., 28.
70. Thiel, *Nonfoundationalism*, 37.
71. Schults, *The Postfoundationalist Task*, 39.

ment with van Huyssteen,[72] builds on these key insights. Although I will later take the implications of van Huyssteen's postfoundationalist thinking in a different direction than Müller, I still share many of his affinities with van Huyssteen. This can be seen in the affirmation and importance of the local context[73] and the value of cross-disciplinary research (specifically a transversal approach[74]). Both of these have been enormously important in the development of practical theology (these will be discussed later) and continue to be. A postfoundationalist approach will affirm this and hopefully provide new insights.

In order to best articulate this middle way Schults has attempted to develop four couplets to describe an *ideal* postfoundationalist perspective.[75] I will briefly examine each of the four while discussing their relevance for practical theology and how they will be taken up later.

1. *Experience and belief: interpreted experience engenders and nourishes all beliefs, and a network of beliefs informs the interpretation of experience.*

Experience here can appear confusing. Schults equates experience as the foundationalist idea that basic beliefs can be either conceptual or sensual (rationalist or empiricist).[76] The foundationalist "sneaks" in these basic beliefs to build on knowledge and to engage with the world accordingly. The nonfoundationalist rightly questions this fallacy and argues that one can only have a web of belief that influences how we see things, and that this web would obviously be relative. It is relative because one's experience

---

72. For a deeply personal account of how van Huyssteen influenced his theological journey towards postfoundationalism see Müller, "HIV/AIDS," 293–306.

73. Müller (ibid.) uses van Huyssteen's emphasis on contextuality and interpreted experience and makes a direct link to its relevance to practical pheology in three areas. Whereby a 1) specific context is described; 2) in context experiences are listened to and described; 3) and interpretations of experiences are made, described and developed in collaboration with co-researchers. These themes will be picked up later in the discussion regarding methodology and the importance of the local and contextual dimensions within practical theology.

74. I will be discussing this in more detail when I discuss the cross-disciplinary dimension in practical theology. Suffice to say van Huyssteen sees transversal rationality, influenced by Schrag, as crucial for a postfoundationalist approach. Both Osmer (*Practical Theology*, 170–72) and Müller ("Practical Theology") have begun to explore the value of this approach for practical theology.

75. Schults, *The Postfoundationalist Task*, 43.

76. Ibid., 44.

with the world can only be mediated by this web of belief. Schults now proposes we move beyond the two options of relativity and certainty. We move beyond certainty by affirming that all beliefs (whether empirical or rationalist) are interpreted already. We come with a belief system that is interpreted experience, and hence fallible. The foundationalist anxiety that these webs of belief are divorced from the world is overcome by affirming that just because one's experience of the world is interpreted does not mean it is in fact false. There are ways we can make judgements about which web of belief is a more accurate interpretation of that reality. Schults points directly to van Huyssteen's use of critical realism as a way of affirming the embedded nature of knowledge and belief (critical) without affirming its irrationality (realism).[77]

2. *Truth and knowledge: the objective unity of truth is a necessary condition for the intelligible search for knowledge, and the subjective multiplicity of knowledge indicates the fallibility of truth claims.*

The dichotomy here is obvious. Can we know truth or are all things relative? Here Schults argues that we ought to keep the quest for truth and the intelligibility of our beliefs without trying to force them into some kind of grand metanarrative or absolutizing our views. He argues that we ought to affirm the realist intuitions of our Christian faith without falling into a kind of fideism or foundationalism that roots our belief in sure foundations of the word of God (whether understood in the infallible or the Barthian sense) or subjective religious experience (Schleiermacher). It is a fallibilist knowledge, yet one that believes in the quest for truth and the possibility that truth can be known. Again, Schults points to van Huyssteen and his affirmation of critical realism in order to bolster this middle way.[78] "Critical" affirms the contextual and fallibilist nature of our knowledge, while "realism" affirms the fact that we are talking about real things that can be known.

3. *Rational judgment is an activity of socially situated individuals, and the cultural community indeterminately mediates the criteria of rationality.*

Foundationalism has sought a contextual and universal criteria that technically would be available to any given individual devoid of context.

77. Ibid., 46.
78. Ibid., 50–51.

Nonfoundationalism has rightly described and critiqued this venture as impossible. Our *web of beliefs*, here seen as the *tradition of a community* entraps us. This makes objective knowledge of an individual impossible, making all knowledge not only contextual but also relative. Postfoundationalism, according to Schults, helps us move beyond these false theoretical concepts. It affirms the reality that the individual is, of course, naturally formed by a specific tradition. It however allows the individual subject the ability to stand outside of that tradition and critique it. This to-and-fro motion between individual and community takes both the positives, while disposing of the negatives of foundationalism and nonfoundationalism. Critical for the individual as part of a given communal tradition is to be able to engage in cross-disciplinary endeavors. This is possible due to, and recalling the title of one of van Huyssteen's books, the shared resources of rationality. This enables us to further transcend the extreme forms of relativism found in many forms of nonfoundationalism. The relevance of this for practical theology cannot be overstated, and indeed is in reality affirmed. A transversal approach to cross-disciplinary thinking will be explored later as a way of taking further postfoundational insights for practical theology.

4. *Explanation and understanding: explanation aims for universal, transcontextual understanding, and understanding derives from particular contextualized explanations.*

This last couplet discussed by Schults builds on the previous one but takes it further. The foundationalist, in affirming transcontextual knowledge available to the individual apart from communal traditions, believed its understanding of the world and knowledge as universal. The nonfoundationalist however, rightly questioned that but moved to the extreme where its knowledge and understanding was locally and contextually bound, unable to provide knowledge and insight into other domains. Postfoundationalism is able to move beyond this false dichotomy by affirming with the nonfoundationalist that all understandings of reality are contextually and locally placed. They are, however, not bound. All explanations of reality are in fact universal in intent. Again, cross-disciplinary work becomes crucial. It does not fall into the trap of necessarily claiming universal knowledge but seeks through transversality (as opposed to universality) to approach better approximations of the truth. Through various explanations, from a variety of disciplines, a more accurate picture of any given situation emerges based on the shared resources of rationality.

These four couplets provided by Schults enable us to see the contours of a postfoundationalist perspective: the tension between our experience of the world and the web of beliefs we use to interpret that experience; the importance of truth and the fallibility of knowledge; the problem of rationality of the individual and the community that the individual is a part of; the relevance of our explanations beyond our community, despite its contextuality.

What emerges from this discussion is both the affirmation that we actually do experience the real world, but through the interpreted experience of our beliefs. Therefore it is interpreted experience. We can seek true knowledge, but one that always retains a fallibilist perspective due to its contextuality. This contextuality of any given community does not nullify individual judgements and rationality, which can in turn influence communal discussions. This contextuality limits our understanding but does not mean that our explanations of reality cannot be universal in intent. A transversal cross-disciplinary discussion now becomes apparent.

The hermeneutical circle becomes a direct expression of the tension between experience and knowledge. The value of the local and contextual nature of practical theology comes into stark relief with the affirmation of local knowledge. The importance of cross-disciplinary thinking is affirmed as vital in the quest for true knowledge that might be relative yet still universal in its intent for explanation. The discussion about postfoundationalism does shed light on the question of methodology in practical theology (hermeneutical circle), the importance of practice as the starting point (local and contextual), as well as affirming the importance of cross-disciplinary thinking (theoretical engagement).

Postfoundationalism also offers us more when we begin to understand critical realism and its relation to postfoundationalism. If the above discussion mapping the contours of a postfoundationalist approach describes *what* the various tensions look like, a critical realist method now describes *how* these tensions are kept in place. Critical realism will also provide the necessary framework for how we engage with the relevant sources at a cross-disciplinary level.

CRITICAL REALISM

Van Huyssteen cautions regarding certain aspects of nonfoundationalism. Thiel notes the very real concern that critics of nonfoundationalism have, that nihilism is the outcome of nonfoundationalism, and that this epistemic relativism is logically self-defeating.[79] Van Huyssteen highlights extreme forms of nonfoundationalism that certainly do imply what seems to be a "total relativism of rationalities."[80]

In a very important essay entitled "Critical Realism and God: Can there be Faith after Foundationalism," published in his book *Essays in Postfoundationalist Theology*, van Huyssteen argues that critical realism could indeed be our way forward beyond foundationalism. What he questions with regard to Christian faith, we might ask with regard to practical theology:

> Can there be a life of committed Christian faith after moving beyond the absolutism of foundationalism and the relativism of antifoundationalism? I believe a plausible, and very helpful, postfoundationalist model for theistic belief can be found in a carefully constructed critical realism. After all, the model of rationality we choose to live by very much determines our intellectual context.[81]

It could be perceived that there is a rush to jump on the critical realism bandwagon. Alistair McGrath has committed himself to critical realism and is strongly influenced by Roy Bhaskar in this regard.[82] New Testament scholars such as Ben Meyer and N. T. Wright[83] have also used critical realism as a way to describe their approaches.

The phrase "critical realism," although widespread today, has its origins in the work of R. W. Sellars. His published work in 1916 was entitled *Critical Realism: A Study of the Nature and Conditions of Knowledge*. Today one can find critical realist reflections on economics, education and politics.[84]

Van Huyssteen's challenge to take critical realism seriously must be taken up. Van Huyssteen produced an entire book[85] early on in his career, but as Osmer[86] has counseled, he should learn from developments since

---

79. Thiel, *Nonfoundationalism*, 81.
80. van Huyssteen, *Essays in Postfoundationalist Theology*, 3.
81. Ibid., 41.
82. McGrath, *A Scientific Theology*, 195–96.
83. Wright, *The New Testament*, 32.
84. See, Patomaki, *After International Relations*; Scott, *Education*; Fleetwood, *Critical Realism*.
85. van Huyssteen, *The Justification of Belief*.
86. Osmer, "Transversal Model," 344.

then. He points to the work of Roy Bhaskar as one who would prove particularly helpful in this regard.

Bhaskar has been at the forefront of recent discussions of critical realism. He notes that in fact critical realism has been practiced for centuries, if not millennia, and it is this rationality that he is trying to bring out.[87] Collier believes that his contribution to critical realism has been the "most original and influential."[88]

Distinctive to Bhaskar's approach is a move away from positivism as the dominant way of understanding the sciences.[89] Central to this approach for Bhaskar was towards a view that held, "(1) the social character of science and (2) the independence from science of the objects of scientific thought."[90] This is a view that takes into account many of the couplets that I discussed previously of Schults. It affirms the reality of the world we observe while noting the local, contextual and fallibilist nature of our reflections. In Bhaskar's terms it moves beyond transcendental idealism and empiricism. It is perhaps for this reason that Bhaskar refers to his position as "not foundationalist."[91] Collier puts it slightly differently but with the same emphasis: "it recognizes that science is about something, and about something that exists independently of the science; and as fallibilist, it recognizes that the science of any given time can be wrong about its object."[92]

Flowing from this critical realist approach is the affirmation of ontology (the way the world is) as prior to our epistemology (what we can know of the world). This leads to the acknowledgment that the world, as it has evolved, has done so in a stratified manner. Therefore we use different methods to understand different dimensions of reality. But it is the same reality. McGrath comments that the relationship between ontology and epistemology and how that ought to be approached is: "through the notion of stratification, which plays a particularly important role in the form of critical realism developed by Bhaskar. If it is conceded that ontology determines epistemology—a fundamental principle of Bhaskar's approach—

---

87. Bhaskar and Hartwig, *The Formation of Critical Realism*, vii.
88. Collier, *Critical Realism*, ix.
89. Bhaskar, *A Realist Theory of Science*, 1.
90. Ibid., 14.
91. Bhaskar and Hartwig, *The Formation of Critical Realism*, 81.
92. Collier, *Critical Realism*, 50.

it follows that the distinct characteristics of each emergent level demand its own characteristic mode of engagement and representation.[93]"

For Bhaskar this means that the social sciences as well as the natural sciences study different dimensions of ontology. The specific research tradition that one finds oneself a part of adds a *double specificity* to this process.[94] I can see the obvious benefits here of a transversal approach that moves between various sciences in terms of providing a more revealing picture of ontological reality.

Perhaps this is why Osmer has encouraged van Huyssteen to engage more strongly with Bhaskar and how one can make truth claims in a transversal approach in interdisciplinary engagement.[95] We are talking about the same reality, but perhaps in different strata and from different research paradigms. The resources of rationality apply to all dimensions and therefore a transversal approach gains much from Bhaskar's ontological argument.

The critical realist approach of both van Huyssteen and Bhaskar have many similarities as Osmer notes:

> They affirm the fallibilism of all truth claims, on the one hand, but make judgements about the relative adequacy of the truth of particular theories in terms of their explanatory power, on the other. Some perspectives are, in fact, more truthful than others because they better explain the generative mechanisms and contingencies in the working of natural and social phenomena.[96]

Central to the fallibilist approach that they both argue for is the role of language. Much of our discussion regarding postmodernism and postfoundationalism focuses on the complexity of language and how it represents reality. Not only is language flawed by its contextual nature, but it is also burdened by the fact that neither reason nor experience can provide a sure-proof foundation of the reality to which language purports to represent. However, van Huyssteen makes the bold statement that our language can represent reality in some ways.[97] But, the critical realist approach realizes that our language is an indirect account of the given reality. It is, therefore, referential, and analogical. Most importantly, it is critical in the sense that

---

93. McGrath, *A Fine Tuned Universe*, 214.
94. Bhaskar and Hartwig, *The Formation of Critical Realism*, 76–77.
95. Osmer, "Transversal Model," 344.
96. Ibid.
97. van Huyssteen, *Essays in Postfoundationalist Theology*, 43.

it always maintains a sense of openness and provisionality throughout the process.

Critical realism then attempts to take the separation between reality and our ability to simply reproduce it in exact fashion, seriously. It agrees that there is indeed a separation between reality and our knowledge of it. Yet, at the same time it believes, like naïve realism, that we can have knowledge that can be true.[98] We can make "reliable cognitive claims."[99]

This essentially is a mediating position between naïve realism on the one hand and phenomenalism on the other. Naïve realism is that form of knowledge taken up strongly during modernism by foundationalist philosophers, that the mind can know the world exactly, exhaustively, and without bias. Knowledge and reality are equated uncritically.[100] Osmer notes that the defining feature of critical realism is that "it rejects the simple correspondence theory of truth found in naïve realism."[101] Critical realism sets "limits to the range of religious and theological language" that we can achieve.[102]

On the other hand, phenomenalism believes that the only thing we can know for certain is the sense experience we have of the raw data around us[103] and emphasizes a distinction between this data and our ability to understand it. Phenomenalism can find expression in various forms of instrumentalism or determinism.[104]

Critical realism believes the world out there is real and we can know it in a provisional sense. However, the critical dynamic requires of us to acknowledge that: "the only access we have to this reality lies along the spiralling path of appropriate dialogue or conversation between the knower and the thing known. . . . This path leads to critical reflection on our reality, so that our assertions about reality acknowledge their own provisionality."[105]

Osmer makes the following comments with regard to research in practical theology and critical realism: "Empirical research, thus does not claim to offer direct access to natural and social objects, for it is informed

---

98. Hiebert, *Anthropological Reflections*, 25.
99. van Huyssteen, *Essays in Postfoundationalist Theology*, 44.
100. Hiebert, *Anthropological Reflections*, 23.
101. Osmer, *Practical Theology*, 74.
102. van Huyssteen, *Essays in Postfoundationalist Theology*, 51.
103. Wright, *The New Testament and the People of God*, 34.
104. Hiebert, *Anthropological Reflections*, 22.
105. Wright, *The New Testament and the People of God*, 35.

by particular (and relative) theories. Rather, empirical research interacts with theory, testing, revising, and elaborating its perspectives. It is the interaction of empirical research and theory that leads to the formation of more adequate explanation of the natural social world."[106]

Postmodernism, Nonfoundationalism, and Critical Realism

By examining postmodernism, nonfoundationalism and critical realism, the various insights, concerns and proposals that have emerged from the discussion will be brought to bear on our engagement with practical theology as a discipline. Now we shall begin to explore practical theology itself, its historical development, and we'll define its terms. In concluding this section, a quote from van Huyssteen,[107] which best illustrates the relationship between postmodernism, nonfoundationalism, and critical realism, has been chosen:

> The key to moving to a postfoundationalist position that moves beyond the alternatives of foundationalism and antifoundationalism lies not in radically opposing postmodern thought to modernity, but in realizing that postmodern thought shows itself in the constant interrogation of foundationalist assumptions and this in always interrupting the discourse of modernity. . . . In fact, when postmodern thought challenges foundationalist assumptions in theology, a fallibilist, experiential epistemology can develop that is highly consonant with the qualified form of critical realism that I have been proposing.

---

106. Osmer, *Practical Theology*, 74.
107. van Huyssteen, *Essays in Postfoundationalist Theology*, 49.

THREE

Practical Theology

Whatever good things may be said about, and from the perspective of, practical theology, it does not really have a clear image of its own

—JACOB FIRET.[1]

Modern practical theology had its beginnings in the 1960s. Since then a considerable consensus has emerged regarding the view that practical theology is a theological theory of action . . . within a theology that is understood as a practice orientated science

—GERBEN HEITINK.[2]

The above two quotes (both from Dutch practical theologians from the Free University in Amsterdam) are taken from Firet's magisterial work *Dynamics in Pastoring*, first published in 1968, as well as Heitink's well-known *Practical Theology: History, Action and Domains*, first published in 1993. The reason for the juxtaposition of the two quotes (despite the helpful fact of being from the same university and nation), is to show just how far practical theology has moved in the past few decades. From a discipline struggling to define itself and let go of its historical baggage in the 1960s, to a discipline that is diverse yet has arrived at some general sense of what it is—now being accepted within the theological fraternity in its own right. Though the reasons for this differ according to the context practical theol-

1. Firet, *Dynamics in Pastoring*, 1.
2. Heitink, *Practical Theology*, 104.

ogy finds itself in, as well as its area of focus.³ It is a field truly coming into bloom.⁴ Of course, in the early 1990s things have moved on from Heitink and, as the editors of the compendium of essays that practical theologians published as *Blackwell Reader in Pastoral and Practical Theology* note, the discipline is always "moving, changing and adapting."⁵ Even the last decade has seen an enormous amount of material that continues to shift the direction of the discipline at large. The *Wiley Blackwell Companion to Practical Theology* notes this. In the introduction Miller-McLemore states that "practical theology has grown to such an extent that there is a serious need to clarify its emerging uses and contributions."⁶ Despite the advances within practical theology, as well as its adaptive and transformative nature, theological reflection (which they use to refer to both pastoral and practical theology in the Blackwell reader⁷) remains elusive, diverse, and controversial. Written as recently as 2006, Graham et al. muse: "Theological reflection is still easier said than done. Received understandings of theological reflection are largely under-theorized and narrow, and too often fail to connect adequately with biblical, historical, and systematic scholarship."⁸ I hope to take up part of this challenge when I look at how critical realism as an expression of postfoundationalism might give us a deeper confidence

---

3. Miller-McLemore ("Clerical Paradigm") argues that it is now a misunderstanding to see practical theology as a marginal discipline, and that this is due to a greater emphasis on practice and its importance in the university (7–13). Schweitzer ("Beyond Misunderstandings") agrees that practical theology is now firmly established but that this has more to do with social and religious changes that have taken place in Germany and not the new-found importance of practice as in the United States. In Australia the situation I would say is far more complex. Practical theology as a disciplinary title is unused in most Protestant circles of which I am a part of. The APTO (Association of Practical Theology in Oceania) of which I am a member is largely Catholic. At our recent annual conference I was one of only three who were not from a Catholic background. This of course by no means implies that practical theology is not taking place (it is), but simply that it is not a well-defined and cohesive discipline in Protestant circles.

4. Moore, "Editorial Practical Theology," 176.

5. Woodward and Pattison, *The Blackwell Reader*, xiv.

6. Miller-McLemore, *Wiley-Blackwell*, 12.

7. When I define terminology at a later stage I will remark just how unhelpful lumping these two terms together can be. Recent discussions have confirmed this to me again. Miller-McLemore (*Wiley-Blackwell*, 16) feels that we need to accentuate the distinction between practical theology and pastoral theology. It does not accurately reflect the diversity and distinct focus of various sub-disciplines within practical theology.

8. Graham et al., *Theological Reflection*, 1.

to engage with other theological disciplines that we have dismissed as irrelevant to practice, or at best only seen as applied theology.[9]

This section, hopes to engage in sufficient detail with practical theology as a discipline, despite this diversity. Those familiar with the historical development of practical theology could easily skip this section and move onto chapter 4 and the discussion of some of the unique contributions of postfoundationalism for practical theology. To those for whom practical theology is relatively new, the next discussion will prove helpful as a general introduction to key terminology and developments within practical theology. What I also hope to achieve in the present section is to show how in many ways practical theology is already functioning within a postfoundationalist pattern. This is seen in its emphasis of the local and contextual as a starting point for theological reflection as opposed to applied forms of theology. Its pastoral cycle also reflects key hermeneutical affinities with postfoundationalism. Cross-disciplinary thinking is also seen as particularly forward thinking in embracing postfoundational concerns. It will be seen that the discipline is certainly still not stuck in its modernistic paradigm of foundationalism and has moved beyond modernism.

Of course, these developments in the field of practical theology have been taking place at the same time as wider developments with regard to the nature of theological education and education itself. With regard to theological education, in his definitive book *Theologia: The Fragmentation and Unity of Theological Education,* Farley makes the sober statement that theological education cannot take place in today's theological schools.[10] I'm not sure I agree with his sentiments.

Kelsey tries to show the various intersecting realities of this debate involving theological education.[11] He believes that theological education is

---

9. Osmer ("The United States," 72) argues for a deeper engagement with other theological disciplines and maintains that practical theology has suffered from thinking of the interdisciplinary task as only between practical theology and sciences that are non-theological. Ward agrees that such a task is indeed important ("The Hermeneutical," 58, 60). He also lamented the fact that practical theology is so fearful of doctrine, or specifically theological statements. Although Ward did not make the direct link between the lack of theological/doctrinal statements in practical theology and the dismissal of other theological disciplines, I believe there is a key link here. My attempt later to use the term "missional" is one such attempt to provide a theological framework to place my reflections on postfoundationalism in theological context. To the extent that I succeed in this, or whether it hinders my argument, I will leave to the reader to decide.

10. Farley, *Theologia,* 14.

11. Kelsey, *To Understand God Truly,* 63.

varied as a result of how we understand the nature of the Christian "thing," how we understand God, what form a theological community should take, and how theological education should actually take place. This debate within theology in general must also be seen in light of the wider developments with regard to education, which has had its effect on theological education, as well as practical theology and theological reflection. This can be witnessed through the rebirth of practical philosophy, which has become influential across a variety of scientific disciplines.[12]

Even within conservative evangelical circles, questions of theological method have become important. *Evangelical Futures: A Conversation on Theological Method,* by some of the leading evangelical scholars, is testament to this. Alister McGrath notes: "We must allow for the fact that many evangelicals have grown up in an intellectual environment that shapes their thinking on how theology is done and have absorbed this without feeling the need to give it formal expression in something as rigorous as theological method."[13]

Already it appears that we might be getting ahead of ourselves. Having noted the interest in theological methodology, the changed and changing face of practical theology, as well as the wider concerns of education, we must now move to delineating these realities more thoroughly and systematically. We will begin by defining terms.

DEFINING TERMS

One would have noticed how, in the preliminary comments on practical theology, three terms found their way into the discussion: being "pastoral theology," "practical theology," and "theological reflection." Authors in practical theology often use the terms interchangeably, which then makes understanding difficult. What is more difficult is when authors have very different understandings of what these words mean and use them in a very intentional manner to communicate something. Therefore, I hope to bring some clarity to this while making it clear in what way I understand and use these terms. As will become apparent, I prefer to use the term "practical theology" when referring to the discipline itself, and "theological reflection" when referring to the actual practice of doing theology in the church and world.

12. Browning, *A Fundamental Practical Theology,* 34.
13. McGrath, "Evangelical Theological Method," 16.

Pastoral Theology

The *Blackwell Reader in Pastoral and Practical Theology*, published in 2000, has pastoral theology alongside practical theology in its title. The point being that although practical theology has become generally accepted as defining this particular discipline in relation to the other disciplines (i.e., biblical studies, church history, etc.), this is not the term used by all. Reader believes distinguishing between pastoral theology and practical theology is fruitless.[14] I disagree and believe that there is an important distinction, although clear overlaps. Louw seems to indicate that pastoral theology forms a part of practical theology.[15] Later, he spends a good portion of his time delineating the hermeneutical dimensions of practical theology, and indeed concludes that "pastoral hermeneutics is a subdivision of practical theology."[16]

So, what is pastoral theology then? Certainly, the term is older than practical theology and is often referred to as the need to guide, heal, reconcile, and sustain the Christian community.[17] The term is still used frequently in the Catholic tradition.[18] Cahalan notes that many Catholics today will note the difference between pastoral theology and practical theology, while at the same time still using the terms interchangeably.[19] This is unusual in light of Karl Rahner's preference for the term "practical theology" instead of the more traditional pastoral theology.[20] Of course the term is not unique to the Catholic tradition and has influences from Puritanism, Pietism, and the Reformed tradition.[21] Amongst these traditions today, pastoral theology could be clarified as such: "practical theology has tended to be preferred as a term that includes pastoral theology within the mainstream reformed tradition. Anglicanism, however, has tended to use the concept 'pastoral theology' when talking about theology relating to practical theology."[22] What makes matters more complex is that many

---

14. Reader, *Reconstructing Practical Theology*, 4.
15. Louw, *A Pastoral Hermeneutic*, 4.
16. Ibid., 98.
17. Woodward and Pattison, *The Blackwell Reader*, 1.
18. Ibid., 2.
19. Cahalan, "Locating Practical Theology," 3.
20. Kelty, "Practical Theology in Australia," 150.
21. Hurding, *Root and Shoots*, 17.
22. Woodward and Pattison, *The Blackwell Reader*, 2.

use the term pastoral theology to refer to the term pastoral care. For this and other reasons, many find the term too narrow with its apparent focus on pastoral and church community concerns.[23] Pastoral care, of course, is a broad field in itself. I have chosen two examples to demonstrate what I would consider the limiting nature of the term.

John Patton's book *Pastoral Care in Context* is an interesting case in showing how pastoral theology in many ways means pastoral care. Not once does he mention the term "practical theology" in the book, yet he would certainly fall under the broad field of practical theology and he is professor of pastoral theology at the University of Columbia. This lack of reference to practical theology (neither did he mention pastoral theology much) could be due to the fact that he did not write a book about theology, but chose to focus on pastoral care. He states this towards the end of his book, but with the important point that it is vital to reflect theologically on pastoral theology, even though his book did not.[24] His article entitled "Introduction to Modern Pastoral Theology in the United States" is even more revealing. With regard to the development of modern pastoral theology, Patton states that "pastoral care has been an important part of American pastoral theology."[25] He comments that students educated in theological schools are educated in accordance with standards set out by the Association for Clinical Pastoral Education and American Association of Pastoral Counsellors.[26] Donald Capps is one who also seems to indicate the limited nature of the term pastoral care.[27] He is professor of pastoral theology at Princeton and seems to focus largely on pastoral care issues. Of course there is nothing wrong with pastoral care and pastoral theology, which is of vital importance to church life and God's mission in the world. What is being illustrated with regard to Patton and Capps is how pastoral theology should be considered a part of practical theology and not synonymous with the term itself. This might seem unfair when one considers the fact that Ballard, in his article "The Emergence of Pastoral and Practical Theology in Britain," uses the terms "pastoral theology" and "practical theology" interchangeably.[28] However, even he notes that the counseling paradigm

23. Ibid.; O'Brien, "Reconciling Identity," 233.
24. Patton, *Pastoral Care in Context*, 237.
25. Patton, "Introduction," 53.
26. Ibid.
27. Capps, *Living Stories*.
28. Ballard, "The Emergence," 66.

Practical Theology

dominated pastoral and even practical theology in the 1970s and 1980s, and was influenced by the developments in America. However, his freedom to use the terms interchangeably might stem from the fact that the British pastoral and practical theology environment always had a more secular, public, plural, and non-professional side to it.[29] In fact, the title of Ballard's book with Pritchard, *Practical Theology in Action: Christian Thinking in the Service of Church and Society*, says it all. In the book the term "pastoral theology" falls by the wayside and "practical theology" becomes the preferred term. Here, practical theology can involve issues dealing with anything from the environment to "every aspect of social policy and cultural experience."[30]

Despite what might seem as so vast a distinction that is being made here, it is important to note that pastoral theology, like practical theology, is still interested in how theology can be informed, and indeed inform effective Christian response in the world.[31] I do not say that pastoral care and pastoral theology are simply concerned with counseling and do not take wider concerns into account. This broader view can be seen in the excellent work of David Augsburger with his cross-cultural analysis and concern.[32] With regard to the present discussion around pastoral theology, however, I still believe it says something that the British and Irish Association for Practical Theology changed its name from the original title of the British Pastoral Studies Teacher's Conference.[33] My conclusion, therefore, with regard to the term "pastoral theology," and when I use it or reference it from others, is that I choose to place it within the broader field and scope of what is known as practical theology.

Practical Theology

What will be attempted at this point is to give a working definition of practical theology, which will then receive further elaboration and expression when given its historical setting. Trying to define practical theology is difficult. And with the wide range of methods and approaches, Willows and Swinton's comment is apt in noting that one "could be forgiven for

29. Ibid., 67.
30. Ballard and Pritchard, *Practical Theology in Action*, 6.
31. Woodward and Pattison, *The Blackwell Reader*, 2.
32. Augsburger, *Pastoral Counselling across Cultures*.
33. Ballard and Pritchard, *Practical Theology in Action*, 2.

assuming that practical theology is whatever any particular practical theologian says it is!"[34]

Hendricks's work on congregational studies (which he considers a sub-discipline of practical theology), defines practical theology as "a continuing hermeneutical concern discerning how the Word should be proclaimed in word and deed in the world."[35] Cartledge notes that practical theology is a diverse and fragmented discipline, with approaches that could stress either "therapy, mission, liberation and pastoral practice."[36] The editors of the *Series in Practical Theology*, quoted in Heitink, have chosen the following definition:

> Practical theology should be understood as an empirically descriptive and critically constructive theory of religious practice. The empirical and descriptive dimension, which is pursued in close cooperation with other disciplines in the field of cultural studies, prevents practical theology from wishful speculative thinking and contributes to empirical theory building. The critical and constructive dimension, which is aimed at evaluating and improving the existing forms of religious practice, prevents practical theology from empiricism or positivism and contributes to a theology of transformation in the name of true religion. . . . Religious practice may be studied on three different levels: with reference to society and culture, with reference to the church, and with reference to the individual. Christianity is not limited to the church, and practical theology should not be limited to a clerical paradigm. Its threefold focus is on ecclesial practices, on religious aspects of culture and society, and on the religious dimension of individual life, including the interrelatedness of all three.[37]

Broad in Scope

Of course, there is more to practical theology than the above quote suggests, yet it certainly covers some important aspects. Here, the breadth and scope of practical theology ranges from the individual, the church, and then to larger societal-cultural questions. Like the editors mentioned earlier, Hendricks's scope includes the individual but also the ecological

34. Willows and Swinton, *Spiritual Dimensions of Pastoral Care*, 11.
35. Hendriks, *Studying Congregations in Africa*, 19.
36. Cartledge, *Practical Theology*, 3.
37. Heitink, *Practical Theology*, xvi.

dimension.³⁸ On the ecological dimension of practical theology, Daniel Louw, in his book on pastoral care, speaks of the notion of "greening the church."³⁹ He points out the need to take seriously one's concern regarding the environment, which he later notes is the priestly task of sanctifying the earth.⁴⁰ Although one can see the importance of this for the individual within pastoral care, the role of ecology in practical theology has far wider implications. I would argue that ecology itself takes on a sense of God's presence (concepts of immanence and more particularly panentheism) and falls within the realm, concern, and study of practical theology. It forms in, and of, itself a religious dimension of which the extended quote earlier spoke. Here, it is not the place to enter into a discussion of these complex questions with regard to the environment, but simply to point out that the church's record with regard to the environment has been nothing short of abysmal.⁴¹ Van der Ven et al. have argued that nature still remains a neglected theme in practical theology due to the discipline's strong focus on the human dimension.⁴²

Contextual and Interdisciplinary

Alongside the important affirmation of the broad scope of practical theology comes the concern related to its empirical dynamic. It simply must involve research and arise out of real life situations and concerns. This is why a postfoundationalist perspective can be enormously fruitful for understanding present practices within practical theology and help refine them. In his interesting book, entitled *Practical Theology: Charismatic and Empirical Perspectives*, Mark Cartledge agrees with the emphasis on real life situations and concerns: "For practical theology, with its orientation of engagement with real people in real social contexts, the need to use empirical approaches is fundamental to the discipline. Theoretical and abstract discussion also remains essential but they are used primarily in relation to empirical and concrete studies of people."⁴³

---

38. Hendriks, *Studying Congregations in Africa*, 33.
39. Louw, *A Pastoral Hermeneutic*, 110.
40. Ibid., 119.
41. Basney, *An Earth-Careful Way of Life*, 16.
42. Van der Ven et al., "Nature," 43.
43. Cartledge, *Practical Theology*, 11.

Postfoundationalist Reflections in Practical Theology

Just prior to this quote in the text, Cartledge argued for a close relationship between the social sciences and practical theology.[44] The editors of the *Series in Practical Theology* had mentioned the importance of the cultural sciences as partners to practical theology. One might argue that an attempt to engage with the other sciences makes the practical theologian's task almost an impossibility—at least by itself. Firet notes that in theory a practical theologian would have to be an "exegete, systematic theologian, psychologist, and sociologist . . . to say nothing of historical research."[45] Of course, one could add to this: skills in ethics, church history, economics, politics, and ecology! Despite these difficulties, we need to affirm the dialogical and correlational partner of the social sciences for practical theology. Indeed, van Huyssteen[46] argues that interdisciplinary engagement is vital for theology as a whole in its move beyond foundationalism. One could argue that practical theology itself, by its very nature, is well placed to move beyond foundationalism because of the importance it affords various other disciplines and its wide scope. However, one must not be overawed by the social sciences and must take serious consideration of its potential weaknesses. Much of social science is charged with its own ideology and is not even aware of its own values.[47] Both theological and social science's concerns must be aware of their hermeneutical character—their own *religious* and hidden perspectives.[48] The descriptive nature remains important, but must take these checks into account.

What the earlier quote perhaps did not make clear, but hinted at, was the correlational dimension between theology and human sciences that must take the form of a critical engagement. By *critical* is meant that after the *pastoral concern*[49] has been identified through the process of attending,[50] which is essentially a posture of listening, one brings into dialogue the traditional concerns from the Christian classics, as well as the present concerns raised by the human and social sciences. This correlational dialogue must remain open and feel the risk of possible revision—even on the Christian

---

44. Ibid.
45. Firet, *Dynamics in Pastoring*, 10.
46. van Huyssteen, *Essays in Postfoundationalist Theology*, 34–38.
47. Browning, *A Fundamental Practical Theology*, 81.
48. Ibid., 92.
49. Whitehead and Whitehead, *Method in Ministry*, 13.
50. Ibid., 21.

side.[51] What form of the Christian classics and its tradition becomes the dialogue partner is of course also hotly contested.[52] At this point, and taking into account the preceding discussion, as well as comments which I will make at a later stage, I make the following tentative definition of a postfoundationalist practical theology:

> A postfoundationalist practical theology is a reflection on the given life experiences of people in their individual, church, societal and ecological dimensions that is both missional and glocal. It is therefore both local and contextual consistent with a fallibilist epistemology. Its reflection is intentional and arises out of practice moving into dialogue with the Christian classics (in plurality and ecumenically) and with the human, social and even natural sciences that takes into account the concerns of a nonfoundational epistemology in its approaches to both poles. A transversal approach best elucidates this correlationality, highlighting shared sources of rationality, allowing it to move beyond relativism. This results in a decision for change, which ends up where its reflection started off—practice and mission.

Theological Reflection

One might wonder what difference there is between practical theology and the term that will now be described as *theological reflection*. The short answer to that question is, "not much!" Yet, as one digs a little deeper there are some distinctions that are important to highlight, and they are the distinctions envisaged when using the term. The previous concluding paragraph obviously indicates a very specific view of practical theology—indeed, one with which not everyone would agree. In fact, the truth is that all Christians are engaged in a form of theological reflection, even if they have never heard of the discipline practical theology. We are all familiar with the much bandied about comment in churches that *theology is dangerous*, which is widespread and deep. Of course, this aversion to theology masks the fact that, in some sense, we are all theologians. Grenz and Olson describe this in the following manner:

> A misconception is growing among Christians that a great gulf exists between ordinary Christians and theologians. For some

51. Graham et al., *Theological Reflection*, 168.

52. Ibid., 167.

Postfoundationalist Reflections in Practical Theology

that perceived gap creates fear; for others it creates suspicion and resentment. We want to close the gap by showing that everyone—especially every Christian—is a theologian and that every professional theologian is simply a Christian whose vocation is to do what all Christians do in some way: think and teach about God.[53]

All Christians want to understand God better and to figure out if their faith has any application to the reality in which they find themselves. Despite the exciting situational theology that emerges from this form of theological reflection, it can often remain narrow and polemical. The great fascination with Tim LaHaye's novels of the end times and his series, *Left Behind*, demonstrates this. It creates a fascination with leaving this earth and propagates a brand of pre-millennial theology that is unreflective and escapist. This form of theology has practical consequences on how we view our lives as humans, our planet, and what we choose to do about it. The pitfalls of this form of theological reflection leads to a pessimistic view of the world and a lack of real interest to create change within it.[54] This, of course, is just one example of the negative aspect of theological reflection. The point intended to be made, however, is that it is a uniquely human quest to reflect (whether critically or uncritically) on who we are in relation to God and our situation. Of course, this is not a modern phenomenon of the human race, but in fact is as old as our species itself. In his book, *The Story of God*, Robert Winston demonstrates that, from the very beginning, our earliest ancestors reflected on their life experience and its relation to God and the planet—perhaps not in a technical manner of course, but reflection nonetheless.[55] It is of interest that, toward the end of his book, *Theologia*, where he calls for the recovery of the understanding of *theologia*, Farley notes: "Although the understanding of the believer may result from a self-conscious effort, this does not mean technical scholarship. It is the understanding required by the life of faith in the world. This mode of understanding is reflection or theological reflection."[56]

Graham et al. attempt to track the many and varied ways that theological reflection has taken place within the Christian tradition—in technical and nontechnical ways. They list seven ways, with examples from original source material, to demonstrate this process of theological

---

53. Grenz and Olson, *Who Needs Theology?*, 13.
54. Grenz, *The Millennial Maze*, 146.
55. Winston, *The Story of God*, 22.
56. Farley, *Theologia*, 157.

reflection. "Christian ministry comes to be understood as being less about the application of expertise and more about facilitating the vocation of all Christians through processes of understanding, analysing and reflecting. The purpose of theological education, therefore, is to equip people with skills and strategies to enable them to reflect theologically."[57] Reader argues for this strongly and contends that: "At a time when far greater emphasis is being placed on the role of the laity in the ministry of the church, it is surely vital that we begin to investigate how doing theology might become a shared local activity."[58]

This desire to help all Christians reflect theologically is not new. This is evident in the many Bible study courses and other theological programs offered in many of our churches today. My personal experience over the last twelve years of my life has been interesting in this regard. Three different denominational groupings each had their own systematic theology that formed the basis of their theological reflection—these being Louis Berkhoff, Wayne Grudem, and Millard Erickson[59] respectively. Characteristic of all these approaches is the form of applied foundationalist theology that has dominated practical theology from the time of Schleiermacher to the 1970s, and, if Farley is correct, even in the early Christian centuries and the Middle Ages.[60] Recently Grab has disputed the fact that Schleiermacher proposed a form of applied theology.[61] Even so, I believe, still with Schleiermacher we have a narrow view of practical theology that focuses on church leadership. Even Grab admits that with Schleiermacher "The practical life of the church and of Christians within it, is not yet practical theology."[62] It also remains for Schleiermacher of central importance that practical theology distils the essence of Christianity. An illustration of this shift and change in practical theology will take place under the historical discussions that will follow later. However, a brief comment is called for here with regard to this applied theology and the call for all within the church to reflect on theology. Applied theology is basically another way of

---

57. Graham et al., *Theological Reflection*, 5.
58. Reader, *Local Theology*, 1.
59. Berkhoff, *Systematic Theology*; Grudem, *Systematic Theology*; Erickson, *Christian Theology*.
60. Farley, *Theologia*, 33–34.
61. Gräb, "Practical Theology," 187.
62. Ibid., 186.

saying foundationalist theology, and an approach to the Bible as the only source for theology, which is also inerrant and captive to foundationalism.[63]

This applied theology approach in many of our churches today is highlighted when adults are invited to begin theological reflection and to come with the idea and belief that they ought to start off by "believing theology to be a set of general rules which they can apply to their lives. They hope to learn these rules and their application so their lives will be better."[64] Despite this, and when theological reflection is encouraged for all Christians, it indeed results in a better embodiment of the gospel and reception of the richness of our Christian heritage.[65] Aside from the applied foundationalist theology model in much of today's theological reflection in our churches, an equal danger lurks in its area of focus. It seems wholly ecclesial in its dimension, and overly individualistic in its application. This is why it will be argued later that a missional approach to theological reflection— which encompasses all of God's world as a dimension of reflection and that values the non-ecclesial worlds of the majority of the church's members—is of vital importance. This is also crucial in emphasizing cross-disciplinary thinking within practical theology, consistent with a postfoundationalist approach. Without pre-empting what will come, a truly missional practical theology will be one that is contextual, springing from experience, and therefore moving beyond foundationalism that makes universal claims, based on "unquestionable" foundations, then applied to a variety of contexts. This is not to make experience some form of certain foundation, but rather give it its unique place in the theological discussion. Experience is open to critique and vulnerable to the limits of knowledge and the limits of context.

Guder notes the importance for each person to identify their calling and gifts and the need for "biblical and theological training to incarnate the Gospel in their particular fields, and then to commission them to that ministry."[66] This missional dimension for practical theology and theological reflection will be dealt with later in evaluating whether it truly represents a move beyond foundationalism.

My view is that theological reflection, in many ways, is similar to practical theology. In an academic setup, one who engages in practical theology

---

63. Benson, "Theology and (Non)(Post) Foundationalism," 68–69.
64. Whitehead and Whitehead, *Method in Ministry*, 103.
65. Ibid., 110.
66. Guder, *The Continuing Conversion*, 178.

in many ways engages in theological reflection. However, theological reflection is in fact an approach in which every human is engaged. All Christians engage in theological reflection—whether they admit it or not. The theological reflection I will argue for is one that seeks to engage God, the world, and ourselves in a reflective and critical manner. The specifically nonfoundational nature of this form of theological reflection will become evident as we progress.

HISTORICAL CONSIDERATIONS

Having taken some time to define the terms that will be used, our discussion with regard to placing ourselves in a historical setting can now begin. As has been mentioned already, theological reflection has a long history that, in fact, goes right back to the beginning of humankind. It is part of being human to reflect theologically on our world and its relation to something other than ourselves. Prior to the time of the early church we have the people of Israel who reflected on their world in relation to God. Later to Paul, who did his theological reflection in the first century, through to the early church fathers, to the councils, through the Middle Ages, to the Enlightenment and our modern world, Christians have been engaging in theological reflection.

The Fragmentation of Theology

Edward Farley argues that, for a long time, theology was seen as the "individual cognition of God and things related to God"—a habit of the human soul known as *habitus*. The second form of theology is a "self-conscious scholarly enterprise of understanding,"[67] which has a more disciplinary twist and can be called *scientia*. Of course, the term "theology" only arose quite late in the Christian tradition, but this habit of the heart and theological reflection existed from the beginning. It would be unwise to say that theological reflection was done in a certain way in the early church, that it changed in the Middle Ages, then morphed again during the Reformation, and then again with Schleiermacher and then with further changes in the twentieth century. That would assume that there was a clear trajectory that can be followed and traced with neat divisions, moving from one form

---

67. Farley, *Theologia*, 31.

of theological reflection to another. Indeed, it is true that there have been changes—and some dramatic. It will be argued later that the second half of the last century witnessed just such a change within theological reflection, or more specifically practical theology. On the whole, however, it is perhaps better to say that forms of theological reflection often ran alongside one another in the church's history. The book by Graham et al., already mentioned, demonstrates this well. Therein, they identify seven various methods of theological reflection and examine ways throughout the church's history that they have been practiced.

This could be paralleled to the reality that Kelsey notes with regard to theological schools.[68] Here, the different ways of understanding God shape the theological school and its form of reflection. Farley examines theology's history throughout the ages from the first few centuries, through the Middle Ages and ending in the Enlightenment.[69] In these periods, *scientia* and *habitus*, although running concurrently, have maintained their essence. With the arrival of the Enlightenment, theology as *habitus* disappears, and *scientia* fragments into various disciplines.

Practical Theology as Applied Theology

In the wake of the Enlightenment and with the arrival of Friedrich Schleiermacher, practical theology as a discipline first began to take shape. The approach that developed at this point defined practical theology right up until the past century and, in fact, still broods over the discipline today. The change that took place during, and after, the Enlightenment has been called the "most important event and the most radical departure from the tradition in the history of education of clergy."[70] The Enlightenment of the subject led Schleiermacher to a radical rethinking of theology. Heitink comments on this development by noting: "practical theology owes its origin to Schleiermacher, the first modern theologian, who, recognizing the value of the Enlightenment, wanted to build a bridge to modern humanity by reflecting on the Christian faith on the basis of the experience of the subject."[71]

68. Kelsey, *To Understand God Truly*, 34.
69. Farley, *Theologia*, 44.
70. Ibid., 49.
71. Heitink, *Practical Theology*, 19.

Practical Theology

Of course, Schleiermacher has been crowned the father of many ideas in theology, of which practical theology is just one. There were others who preceded him and influenced him, such as Gundling and Mosheim,[72] as well as others who sought to embody the practical theological "way" he described, such as C. I. Nitzch.[73] Despite this, today many choose to place Schleiermacher at the starting point of practical theology.[74] What exactly was it that Schleiermacher set into motion that has defined practical theology so dramatically? And what would this have to do with a postfoundationalist practical theology?

Alongside the fragmentation of theology that took place, Schleiermacher's belief that theology should move from historical knowledge to practical application has significant influence. Unfortunately, he did not understand how the church's practices could influence the very questions we bring to our sources.[75] Practical theology now becomes a term for ministry and clergy duties with the sole goal being the application of the theoretical sciences of biblical, historical, and systematic studies.[76] Practical theology itself has simply nothing new to offer philosophical and historical theology.[77] Louw describes this shift in the following manner: "practical theology now becomes applied theology; in other words, the truth is applied to ecclesiastical practice. Focus shifts from clergy's preparation to the functions of the church. This functional approach represents a radical shift which has long term consequences for practical theology."[78]

The process of modernization also led to an empirical shift in society, which has resulted in the rise of the social sciences and sociology in particular.[79] Practical theology has been a bedfellow of empirical studies ever since and, in many ways, is defined by it and cannot avoid it.[80] This is indeed one of its strengths, demonstrating an easy affinity with postfoundationalist thinking, of which cross-disciplinary thinking is vital. Often, however, the

---

72. Farley, *Theologia*, 77.

73. Anderson, *The Shape of Practical Theology*, 24.

74. Heitink, *Practical Theology*, 23; Graham et al., *Theological Reflection*, 2; Woodward and Pattison, *The Blackwell Reader*, 24.

75. Browning, *A Fundamental Practical Theology*, 43.

76. Farley, *Theologia*, 78.

77. Heitink, *Practical Theology*, 26.

78. Louw, *A Pastoral Hermeneutic*, 90.

79. Heitink, *Practical Theology*, 35.

80. Cartledge, *Practical Theology*, 2.

use of the empirical sciences has been accepted uncritically. Browning argues that the social sciences are captive to their own philosophical, ethical, and indeed religious frameworks. However, this does not mean that they should not be embraced by practical theology, but rather that they should function within a specifically theological context.[81] Even van Huyssteen, who argues strongly for the importance of engagement with other disciplines, argues for disciplinary integrity and the importance of standing firm in our traditions.[82]

It was mentioned earlier that practical theology does not move and develop in neat linear lines. This, of course, makes it difficult to analyze how the discipline has been shaped and changed. It was also mentioned earlier that a noticeable shift and change took place in practical theology in the second half of last century as it moved away from the applied theology of the previous century and a half. The fact that this change has taken place is now widely accepted in the practical theological fraternity.[83] There are many reasons that have led to this change in practical theology, some of which will be discussed later. Important to note at this point is that there has been a shift from practical theology being regarded as a fringe discipline within theology, as well as a move away from the view that it focuses on theory and is moved into practice only once all the hard theoretical work is done. It was also often seen in the theological fraternity as practical, but certainly not theological.[84] In the following quote Browning captures this shift delightfully:

> The field of practical theology has been throughout its history the most beleaguered and despised of the theological disciplines. The discipline of theology itself had few friends, even in the church. To admit in academic circles that one is a theologian has been, in recent years, to court embarrassment. To admit that one is a practical theologian invites even deeper scepticism. To admit at a major university that one is a practical theologian has been to invite humiliation. With the rebirth of the practical philosophies, practical theology itself has been reborn. Five years ago few would admit to being practical theologians. Today there is a rush among

---

81. Browning, *A Fundamental Practical Theology*, 92.
82. van Huyssteen, *Essays in Postfoundationalist Theology*, 38.
83. Heitink, *Practical Theology*, 104; Graham et al., *Theological Reflection*, 2.
84. Ganzevoort, "Strange Bedfellows," 1.

more dignified and well-established systematic and historical theologians to ask. After all, aren't we all practical?[85]

The introductory remarks in this section on practical theology mentioned that it was the rise of practical philosophy and practical education that partly explains this shift. Another vastly important factor was the rise of liberation theology, black theology, and feminist theology. Each sought to move from the practice and reality on the ground, examining the stuff of life. People's oppression and their experience becomes a starting point in their theological reflection. One example from James Cone's statement with regard to theological entry points will suffice.[86] He places revelation only fourth in his consideration of doing theology and places Scripture and tradition fifth and sixth. The three sources and starting point for theology are black experience, black history, and black culture. The dramatic impact of this shift will be seen later when the various methodological options with regard to theological reflection are examined. That this focus on a unique context with multiple sources could lead to a postfoundationalist position should be self-evident.

To try to understand this shift in how practical theology has evolved from the 1960s in certain parts of the world to the present will now be examined. As this is being done to demonstrate the shift that has taken place in practical theology as a discipline, an attempt will not be made to paint a picture of practical theology across the world. That is not the goal of this study. The researcher realizes that he focuses strongly on Europe, America, and South Africa in what follows. This does not imply that certain developments outside of these centers are not important. Indeed, the importance of liberation theology in South America has already been referenced. A more sustained interaction with liberation theology will be noted when we engage with methodological issues. The recent work *The Wiley Blackwell Companion to Practical Theology* captures the present state of practical theology in a wide variety of centers, with a wide variety of authors. Indeed it is far more detailed than my short summary to come, which is illustrative of the shift which I am wanting to describe.

---

85. Browning, *A Fundamental Practical Theology*, 3.
86. Cone, *Teologia Nera*, 29.

Developments in Germany

Karl Barth's shadow has continued to hover over the development of practical theology in Germany. This reality left little room for the development of an inductive approach to practical theology.[87] Browning defines Barth's view as practical, only in the sense of applying God's revelation, and he later calls Barth's approach significantly wrong.[88] Bastian believed that Barth contributed to the decline of practical theology.[89] Van Wyk further notes that "Bastian appealed to practical theologians to shake off the chains of dogma and to stand on their own two feet."[90] The normative-deductive approach was rejected, and the need for praxis to correct and critically evaluate theory was stressed. Heitink comments that, with Bastian, one notices an empirical shift that looks for questions that faith evokes, and one that tries to find paths to non-theological disciplines.[91] In 1974, a paper prepared by both Catholic and Protestant practical theologians, entitled "Praktische Theologie heute," was viewed as seminal in breaking the applied theological stranglehold in German practical theology. It showed how practical theology started from concrete praxis and was to be regarded as a theory of action.[92] This path was then followed by others, such as Josuttis and Otto.

Otto lamented practical theology's applied science mentality and neglect of practice. Van Wyk notes that Otto believed:

> theologians have been so busy with their own theological traditions that they have had no time to address contemporary society or the contemporary church. This produced a void in reflection on the relationship between theory and praxis. Further outcomes were a blind emphasis on action, a contentless pastoral praxis, and the establishment of practical theology as an applied science. To overcome these errors, practical theology should take up the premise of its wide social relevance and be redefined in terms of the interrelationship of religion, the church, society, and theology.

---

87. Heitink, *Practical Theology*, 112.
88. Browning, *A Fundamental Practical Theology*, 5 and 7.
89. Heitink, *Practical Theology*, 12.
90. Van Wyk, "Applied Theology," 86.
91. Heitink, *Practical Theology*, 112.
92. Ibid., 113.

Practical theology must be a critical theory of religiously influenced praxis in society.[93]

One of the central figures in German practical theology was Kael Nipkow who was professor of religious education and practical theology at the University of Tubigen from 1968–1995.[94] Following on from the shift from a more hermeneutical approach to a social sciences approach in German education in general in the 1960s, Nipkow believed that the challenges of modern theology, modern education, and modern rationality all had to be taken seriously. He placed high importance on the Bible yet not in the conservative sense or applied theological way.[95] The consequences of much of his thought led to the "demand for a type of religious instruction that takes the contemporary world as its starting point, educationally as well as theologically."[96] Nipkow has his roots in the school of Klafki with its orientation towards the human sciences.[97]

More recent practical theologians in Germany have solidified this shift to a more empirical approach consistent with a shift to the social sciences. Yet Schweitzer still believes many within the theological fraternity still see practical theology or religious education as simply an applicatory discipline. He resists this and places high value on the empirical nature of the discipline and its research.[98] This should not be at the expense of systematic, historical, and comparative research. An example of this comparative research was the work done by himself and Osmer in *Religious Education between Modernization and Globalization.*

Heimbrock also argues strongly for an empirical approach to practical theology. He specifically argues for a phenomenological approach to research. He argues for the importance of taking one's methodological assumptions into account when doing research, and believes a phenomenological approach is one that moves beyond positivistic assumptions of reality.[99]

---

93. Van Wyk, "Applied Theology," 87.
94. Osmer and Schweitzer, *Religious Education*, 192.
95. Ibid., 193.
96. Ibid., 196.
97. Heitink, *Practical Theology*, 271.
98. Schweitzer, "Research in Religious Education," 166 and 167.
99. Heimbrock, "From Data to Theory," 277.

Postfoundationalist Reflections in Practical Theology

Developments in the Netherlands

Of course, in the Netherlands, the name of Jacob Firet dominates in any discussion of practical theology. His book, *Dynamics in Pastoring*, is viewed as seminal in the debate. However, he is met with mixed reception. Heitink seems to speak favorably of him and his development of a theory of action.[100] Others, such as Ballard and Pritchard,[101] view him squarely within the applied theology framework that dominated practical theology for so long. Firet himself states explicitly that practical theology "is not the practical end of the curriculum."[102]

Heitink mentions many other names in Dutch practical theology, such as Haarsma, Kessel, and Hofte.[103] With Van der Ven, he notes a move to an empirical approach, which he defines as fresh. Cartledge credits Van der Ven with breaking new ground and greatly influencing developments in Britain with regard to his empirical theology. He notes the emphasis on practice in Van der Ven, where the "direct object of empirical theology therefore is the faith and practice of people concerned. The social sciences are used to further this enterprise and theology is dependent upon these disciplines within practical theology."[104] Browning notes the effect of practical philosophy on Van der Ven, and indeed even on Firet.[105] Dingemans has noted this shift from applied theology to an investigation of Christian practice itself, and sees both Firet and Van der Ven as examples of this shift to a more empirical approach.[106] Heitink himself would be central to any discussion of practical theology in Holland. Ballard and Pritchard seem to place him alongside Firet as part of the applied theological spectrum.[107] In my view of Heitink, he would question such a perspective and would see him as one who takes the practice of Christian life in the world as of vital importance. In my view, his empirical approach to the mediation of the Christian faith leans toward this.[108] Ganzevoort has shown that Heitink

100. Heitink, *Practical Theology*, 120.
101. Ballard and Pritchard, *Practical Theology in Action*, 62.
102. Firet, *Dynamics in Pastoring*, 11.
103. Heitink, *Practical Theology*, 121.
104. Cartledge, *Practical Theology*, 14.
105. Browning, *A Fundamental Practical Theology*, 35.
106. Dingemans, "Practical Theology in the Academy," 87–88.
107. Ballard and Pritchard, *Practical Theology in Action*, 62.
108. Anderson, *The Shape of Practical Theology*, 25.

attempts to balance empirical, hermeneutical, and strategic concerns in his practical theology.[109]

Developments in Great Britain

Pattison noted that in the 1970s practical theology did not exist as a discipline in England. His studies took him to Edinburgh, which "was then the center of a revival in practical theology as thinking about and analysing experience and theology rather than just teaching ministers how to 'do' practical things like baptising babies."[110] Things have changed since then. Paul Ballard's article "Pastoral and Practical Theology in Britain" notes that practical theology in Britain is one of the fastest growing and most popular areas in the British theological curriculum. He notes that, in times past, the British pastoral scene was dominated by "transferring theological truth into some kind of practice."[111] He further notes that the change that has taken place has been due to the rise of professionalism in ministry and the need to find legitimacy for one's discipline.[112] The crisis of the clergy's role in a declining church has resulted in deep reflection that came with the rapid increase in secularization in the post-war years.[113] Ballard continues by showing that the twentieth century has seen a notable turn to the human in theology, manifested by the various liberationist theologies. It has resulted in a focus on, and the importance of, "lived experience, practice, action and the primacy of human need,"[114] with a move away from abstract theology. The change in the British scene has also been brought about by the turn to the practical in education[115] and a greater awareness of the laity.[116] He sums up the changes in British practical theology with the following words:

> Before the war it was, broadly speaking, a severely practical, atheoretical discipline that was marginal to mainstream theological endeavours and uninformed by the human sciences and professional skills. It was exclusively focussed upon the work of clergy.

109. Ganzevoort, "Forks in the Road," 7.
110. Pattison, *The Challenge of Practical Theology*, 16.
111. Ballard, "The Emergence of Pastoral," 61.
112. Ibid., 63.
113. Ibid., 64.
114. Ibid., 65.
115. Ibid.
116. Ibid., 66.

> Now it is becoming a growing and diverse field which is gradually developing a theoretical literature as well as skills of reflection upon practice of many different kinds. It is gradually moving towards the center of contemporary theological endeavour, as well as outwards to embrace many practical contemporary issues and concerns such as poverty, the future of work, and the nature of community.[117]

The recent work by Cameron et al. has argued strongly for what they call *theological action research* as a vehicle for doing practical theology, consistent with this shift to practice. Action research crops up often in recent work in British practical theology. The professional doctorate in practical theology recently introduced in England is a good example of the changes that have taken place in practical theology. Bennett and Graham discuss the doctorate in the following terms:

> The design and ethos of the PhD certainly accords well with shifts in practical theology itself, which has, over the past two decades, exhibited a shift from an understanding of itself as an "applied" discipline towards a "turn to practice," in which the theorization and analysis of context and practice assume renewed significance, and in which the processes and methods of "theological reflection" on practice are placed at a premium.[118]

This seems to have been a move in the right direction for practical theology in Great Britain. This is confirmed by the study by Lynch and Pattison entitled "Exploring Positive Learning Experiences in the Context of Practical Theological Education" where they sought to examine the experiences of those studying in practical theology institutions, and what they value about the education they have received. The findings confirmed the shift that has taken place within the discipline in Great Britain where the students valued a practical theological education that was relevant to their personal and professional experiences, and gave them the ability to critically reflect on those experiences.[119]

Bennett has noted two growing groups within British practical theology.[120] Both of these groups could provide opportunities for practical

---

117. Ibid., 61.

118. Swinton and Mowat, *Practical Theology*, 255–58; Bennett and Graham, "The Professional Doctorate," 46.

119. Lynch and Pattison, "Exploring Positive Learning," 148–49.

120. Bennett, "Britain," 478–79.

theology to work more closely with the other theological disciplines. The growing Catholic contribution provides a commitment to "systematic and doctrinal issues." The British evangelical community brings with it a distinctive biblical orientation, providing a strong contribution to the "scriptural pole of the hermeneutical circle."

Developments in North America

The pragmatic nature of the American scene has characterized it from the start. This perhaps was the reason why practical theology, as a separate discipline, had no place for such a long time.[121] The influence on pastoral theology early on came in the form of the clinical pastoral movement represented by Seward Hiltner.[122] The most important impact of this movement for practical theology was seen in that:

> Theological reflection on present practice was viewed as having epistemic weight, yielding knowledge that could not be gained by simply reflecting on sacred or academic texts. Such reflection on practice, moreover, was inherently interdisciplinary, bringing theology into dialogue with psychology to make sense of particular contexts.[123]

There was in North America in the 1980s and 1990s "a significant and extended reappraisal of the fundamental aims and purposes of theological education as a whole."[124] This can be seen in the seminal book published in 1983 entitled *Practical Theology: The Emerging Field in Theology, Church and World*. The book captured the changing mood and creative discussion that was emerging at the time. Browning, in his introduction, sought to capture that mood and noted the new interest: "in questions of right action in addition to its traditional interests in right meaning and correct belief. There seems to be a growing hunger to make theology in general more relevant to the guidance of action and to bridge the gap between theory and practice, thought and life, the classic theological disciplines and practical theology."[125]

---

121. Heitink, *Practical Theology*, 115.
122. Patton, "Introduction," 52.
123. Osmer, "The United States."
124. Bass and Dykstra, *For Life Abundant*, 6.
125. Browning, *A Fundamental Practical Theology*, 3.

Heitink[126] notes a shift from pastoral theology to practical theology in the work of Don Browning,[127] who calls for practical theology to begin with practice, then move to theory, with a return to practice. Heitink notes the correlational nature of Browning's theology and discusses the public dimension of Tracy's practical theology. In regard to them, he notes Rebecca Chopp's critique of both Tracy and Browning as being far too academic, modern, and liberal.[128] The major development, which has taken place within North American practical theology, has been the fact that context has been pushed to the forefront, involving the whole situation, background and environment of the specific event and circumstance.[129] In *Teaching Practical Theology: Six Perspectives* we get interesting insight into the present state of practical theology in North America. Here "practice, embodiment, self reflection, and recognition of Gods presence" are important.[130] An extended quote, on reflection on the six perspectives, perhaps best illustrates the present state of North American practical theology:

> Almost all the essays use the term "real" life and directional words like "in" and "out" to describe the subject matter. Meaning only lies "in specific contexts," a location that confounds teaching inevitably abstracted from this. Students must go "out" of the classroom, whether imaginatively through dramatic exercises or literally through ethnographic research that allows a "whiff" of the "air of real situations." Knowledge depends on a practiced ability to "read" these situations and the cultural context around them. It comes from "loving" or "disciplined" attention to the multiple meanings of "what is going on."[131]

There has also been a significant shift to questions around public engagement and life outside the church, which concerns the mission of the church, which is now seen as a legitimate horizon for practical theology in North America.[132]

---

126. Heitink, *Practical Theology*, 118.
127. Browning, *A Fundamental Practical Theology*, 7.
128. Heitink, *Practical Theology*, 118 and 119.
129. Patton, "Introduction," 55.
130. Cahalan et al., "Teaching Practical Theology," 80.
131. Ibid., 81.
132. Cahalan and Nieman, "Mapping the Field," 79.

Developments in South Africa

In the late 1990s Pieterse sketched the situation of practical theology in South Africa by stating that:

> practical theology has been prospering in theological faculties of South African universities since the beginning of the seventies. The discipline is taught and researched at eleven universities of the sixteen in the country. The lecturers in Practical Theology are swamped with post graduate students from all races, many of whom are doing doctoral research. Without overstating it, a person can say that more South Africans obtained doctoral degrees in practical theology in the past three decades than in the whole history of the country.[133]

Pieterse believes the success of practical theology in South Africa was due to the fact that it is essentially a "crisis" discipline suited to South Africa, which has been in a state of "political, economic and social crisis since the sixties."[134] Many theologians have been influenced by this reality in different ways that has led them to their specific approaches. Kretzschmar is one who has argued against a safe descriptive analysis in the academy and for a "theological praxis, in which theory and practice, analysis and action, intellectual development and practical transformation are welded together."[135] It is one that takes "community needs and actions into account."[136] Another example of this was the book published in the late 1980s entitled *Theology and Violence: The South African Debate*. The contributors were from a wide range of disciplines and circles whose theological reflections were based on the contextual realities that were taking place in South Africa at the time.

This contextual nature of practical theology was one of three approaches that Burger had identified in his study on practical theology in South Africa at the time, the others being the *confessional* and *correlational*. Outside of a few exceptions, Burger concluded that not many had reflected on the important questions regarding practical theology. Burger noted that it was only in recent times (late 1980s and early 1990s), that South African practical theologians were beginning to ask methodological questions around the discipline itself. The most notable being that of Pieterse and

---

133. Pieterse, "International Report," 155.
134. Ibid.
135. Kretzschmar, "Ethics in a Theological Context," 20.
136. Kretzschmar, "Introduction," 7.

De Gruchy. Burger stated that with Pieterse there was a notable shift to a more empirical emphasis in practical theology.[137] For Pieterse practical theology is a theory of communicative action, whereby the lifeworlds of individuals and groups come under consideration.[138] Van Wyk believes Pieterse's approach is to "explain, understand and theorise,"[139] through empirical methods, these lifeworlds of communicative action. Pieterse argued that theory and practice ought to be held in tension with regard to the specific "terrain" one studies, and that this terrain ought to be understood empirically.[140]

Pieterse's overview of practical theology in the late 1990s noted Burger's study of practical theology,[141] where he had discussed the three approaches to practical theology in South Africa at the time. With all three approaches Scripture was deemed as important. Pieterse further reflected on Wolfaardt's description of these approaches of Burger's being "Scripture and context, the gospel and context and faith and context." The Scripture and context approach is one where the Bible is used deductively and its contents are sought to be applied to any given context.[142] Van Wyk describes this confessional approach to practical theology in South Africa as follows:

> (1) The study of the Bible is central, and it is the only norm and source of practical theology; W. D. Jonker suggests that practical theology stands in the service of the Word of God? (2) Guidelines for the service of the church are deductively derived from a theological theory based on Reformed theology. (3) The church and the service of the church are central. And (4) the training of ministers is the most important task of practical theology.[143]

The gospel and context approach is seen as a more empirical approach where the Bible is used indirectly and issues in society are taken seriously and not just the church. This more empirical approach is the one of Pieterse's, which we have already noted.

---

137. Burger, *Praktiese Teologie*, 20.
138. Pieterse, *Praktiese Teologie*, 4–5.
139. Van Wyk, "Applied Theology," 93.
140. Pieterse, "Die Metode," 66.
141. Burger, *Praktiese Teologie*.
142. Pieterse, "International Report," 159.
143. Van Wyk, "Applied Theology," 88.

Practical Theology

The last approach is one of faith and context, or Burger's description of a contextual approach.[144] It is one that takes seriously the specific contextual realities within society and seeks their transformation. The Bible is used selectively, and the broader context and religious community are emphasized more than the church. The key work for this approach was that of Cochrane et al., entitled *In Word and Deed: Towards a Practical Theology for Social Transformation*. In it they state that social transformation involved the dismantling of apartheid society and "process whereby society is constructed to be increasingly consonant with the vision and values of the 'Kingdom' or rule of God."[145] In his concluding remarks regarding the various approaches to practical theology in South Africa Pieterse notes a general movement towards the acceptance of a more contextual approach to practical theology:

> To a lesser or greater extent all the theologians are moving towards a contextual theology for praxis. The motivation to develop theories for a transformative praxis has become more urgent. The value of critical theory, social transformation and especially economic transformation of the poor has come to the fore. This is the situation especially as practical theologians want to address the huge social and economic problems of the country and its people. They want to address the praxis and identify the role of the churches in this context. Practical theology, to accept the challenge of its relevancy, will have to approach the challenge reflexively, and fulfil its task close to the actuality of its praxis.[146]

At the same time in the early 1990s there was a significant drive to help local congregations in South Africa reflect on their local context. The handbook by Hendriks, *Strategic Planning in the Congregation: Principles and Practice of Renewal in a Congregation*, became the most used practical theological handbook at the time. Both Hendriks at Stellenbosch and Nel at University of Pretoria sought an "up-building" approach for local congregations instead of the church growth models at the time being pushed from America by the work of McGavran and Wagner. Hendriks work, alongside highlighting the importance of good contextual and congregational analysis, highlighted the importance of the missional and triune dimensions in practical theology. This was done again in *The Future of the Church, the*

---

144. Burger, *Praktiese Teologie*, 161.
145. Cochrane et al., *In Word and in Deed*, 2.
146. Pieterse, "Die Metode," 161–62.

Church of the Future.[147] The same paper highlighted the importance of postmodernism and the growth of African independent and pentecostal churches in South Africa. This focus on the missional and contextual dimensions in practical theology for local congregations was important for Hendriks[148] and was central to his eventual book (widely used not only in South Africa but also in sub-Saharan Africa): *Studying Congregations in Africa*, which discussed his practical theological methodology used in the Network for African Congregational Study (NetACT). This missional shift in congregations is demonstrated in many of the discussions and material on the website.[149]

Also on a congregational level the work of another South African, Wynand De Kock, is important. His Open Seminary methodology and approach to practical theology came to the fore in the early years of 2000. His training of local church leaders to reflect on their local context was influential in many of the Charismatic English-speaking churches. It helps church leaders understand their context, reflect on that context and then lead to transformative action in that context.[150] The methodology has since been used at Tabor College Victoria, Australia, and also at Palmer Seminary in Philadelphia. De Kock comments that: "Openseminary aims to equip leaders for the church who are able to think critically and constructively about the ways in which the church shapes its life to respond to what God is doing in our world. Openseminary networks educational institutions, academics and practitioners to provide graduate level education."[151]

Dreyer has recently argued that there has not been much reflection on the present situation of practical theology in South Africa since Burger and Pieterse.[152] Dreyer, like Pieterse, highlighted the importance of the book *In Word and Deed: Towards a Practical Theology of Social Transformation* as a book that provided an "important outline for a contextual, transformative approach to practical theology" at the time.

Dreyer also highlighted the work of Msomi as an attempt to describe the state of practical theology in the 1990s. Dreyer notes that Msomi

147. Hendriks, "The Future of the Church," 11.
148. Hendriks, "Contextual, Missional Ecclesiology."
149. See www.communitas.co.za
150. De Kock, "Open Seminary at Tabor," 9.
151. De Kock, "Open Seminary."
152. Dreyer, "Practical Theology in SA," 1. See also Burger, *Praktiese* and Pieterse, "International Report."

believed his description was not dissimilar to Burger's. Msomi discusses three approaches—deductive, inductive and dialogical. Dreyer's work then asks the question as to recent developments since the above mentioned studies:

> What has happened since these studies regarding the state of practical theology were published? A few articles or chapters in books have been published in the past decade on specific methodological or epistemological issues or personal approaches to practical theology. . . . I am, however, not aware of a major study on practical theology in South Africa that was done during this period. Perhaps it is time again to take stock of practical theology at the beginning of the second decade of the 21st millennium in the light of recent developments in practical theology on the international scene as well as in our own context.[153]

Dreyer did a short empirical study on the journal *Practical Theology in South Africa* as part of this attempt to describe the present state of practical theology in South Africa.[154] While realizing the limited nature of his choice of journal and other factors, he was able to draw some initial perspectives. The first was that the three approaches that Burger highlighted (confessional, correlational and contextual) are still present. There have however been some further developments, such as a social constructivist as well as a postfoundational narrative approach.[155]

Büchner and Müller have noted that since the 1990s the works of Cas Vos, Pieterse and Julian Müller has become internationally recognized with their hermeneutical and narrative contributions to practical theology.[156] Müller has tried to show the importance of understanding postfoundationalism for practical theology in South Africa, while addressing the important issues of HIV/AIDS. Dreyer mentions new leaders in the field of practical theology such as "Cilliers, Jan-Albert van den Berg, Fritz de Wet, Ian Nell and Gordon Dames."[157]

Dreyer noted that one of the challenges for practical theology is that it had yet to come to terms with the changing reality of the churches in South Africa and the growth of African independent and pentecostal churches.

---

153. Dreyer, "Practical Theology in SA," 2.
154. Ibid., 3–5.
155. Ibid., 4.
156. Büchner and Müller, "The Story," 3.
157. Dreyer, "Practical Theology in SA," 4.

Dreyer also noted that Hendriks has warned the practical theological fraternity of this in 2003.[158]

Dreyer notes that one of the strengths of South African practical theology is its diversity of approaches. Which approach is adopted often depends on which institution one finds oneself in. To end our reflections on South African practical theology a quote from Dreyer describing the apparent unity amongst the diversity of approaches in the country would be apt:[159]

> Is there some agreement on the "core" of practical theology as Ganzevoort (2009) indicated in his paper referred to above? Will we be able to fit most of the work published under the umbrella of "hermeneutics of the cultural approach" and the issue of inter-religiousity that Ganzevoort refers to. It seems to me that most authors still take a more traditional, ecclesiological understanding of the field of practical theology as point of departure, with only a few new and interesting experiments and variations.[160]

In Summary

The above discussion regarding the discipline of practical theology in Europe, America, and South Africa has demonstrated the radical shift that has taken place. Practical theology has moved from a discipline that is focused largely on the end product of theology. It was previously seen as simply the outworking of an applied theology that tells it what it ought to do. With the changes that have taken place a noticeable shift on the importance of reflecting on practice as a starting point for theological reflection has been emphasized. Practical theology has also broadened its concerns from a narrow ecclesial perspective to a more holistic one. This can be seen most obviously in the new emphasis on development research in South African practical theology, which has "broadened the spectrum of practical theological specialization in the socio-economic sphere of life."[161] Of course, this does not mean that now there is some form of methodological consensus.

So much of foundationalism, specifically in its theological guise, has had the quest for sure foundations that lead to certainty and true knowledge.

158. Ibid., 5.
159. Ibid., 6.
160. Ibid., 4.
161. Swart, "Meeting the Challenge," 107.

The postmodern critique and that of the postfoundationalists have poured scorn on this attempt. The shift in practical theology highlighted above in some of the main centers seems be consistent with this shift for a more contextual-based approach, which gives value to local experience. This is consistent with a postfoundationalist approach and should be welcomed. With the growing diversity of sources, and the place of the human sciences finding a voice, there seems to have been a move beyond narrow foundationalist assumptions about how we obtain knowledge and where we obtain it. This is critical in a postfoundational practical theology that values, and perhaps even demands, an interdisciplinary approach.

FOUR

A Postfoundationalist Practical Theology

We started out by examining and comparing a foundationalist and postfoundationalist understanding of reality. Then we moved into a discussion around the development of practical theology and its current state. The tentative conclusion offered was that practical theology has, in many ways, moved beyond foundationalism for the reasons provided in the last section. I now hope to further illumine this by engaging in far greater detail with issues of context and the pastoral cycle under the heading a *glocal praxis-based* practical theology. A detailed discussion of a *critical correlational hermeneutic* will be advanced as an example of how practical theology has indeed moved beyond foundationalism, both in the method itself, but also in its approach to the sources with which the method seeks to engage. At each point though, I will seek to show how postfoundationalist perspectives can provide useful ways to deepen this postfoundationalist turn and provide better ways and reasons for doing practical theology the way it is done. Before doing that, the concept of a *missional* practical theology will be provided, which helps best to get to grips with these issues. It will also become apparent that the broadness of a missional practical theology, in many ways, becomes a way for a postfoundationalist approach to practical theology to be advanced.

Postfoundationalist Reflections in Practical Theology

A MISSIONAL PRACTICAL THEOLOGY

In this section, discussion of the missional nature of practical theology will argue for the importance of this discussion as being integral to any discourse on a postfoundationalist practical theology. Hastings has recently argued that much of practical theology, or certainly its North American dimension, has held onto the hope that some sort of synthesis between the Gospel and Northern American churches and culture might be possible.[1] He believes that only now the question of the mission of congregations is being taken seriously by American practical theologians. Hastings goes on to say that:

> The North American churches are already in a post-Constantinian situation, and a new generation of missional theologians, drawing on the work of Lesslie Newbigin, are wondering whether or not North America can be converted, most practical theologians have still not seriously addressed the hitherto unthinkable problematic of how to understand and guide Christian practice within their own post-Christian social, political, and cultural context.[2]

With the help of David Bosch, an attempt will be made to briefly highlight the problem of missions before trying to place mission in its historical context. Having established these foundations, we will move onto exploring the consequences of the Trinity for a missional practical theology that, in turn, will lead to a missional perspective regarding the nature of the church. In conclusion, the various points and perspectives discussed will be drawn together and argued that an incorrect understanding of mission can lead to a defunct view of practical theology, which could be burdened with foundationalist assumptions. The opposite being that a correct view of mission, critically adhered to and reflected upon, will lead to a healthy practical theology that is broad, holistic, and nonfoundationalist. This will provide the entry point into the section that follows on the local and global nature of practical theology and later to the discussion of postfoundationlism within a correlational hermeneutic.

At this point, the argument is that, at its very root, missional should imply local, contextual, practical and experiential—all things that help us to move beyond foundationalism—and affirm the contextual nature of knowledge and reject forms of applied theology. Again remembering Müller's

1. Hastings, *Practical Theology*, 29.
2. Ibid.

affirmation that practical theology must emphasize these local realities, as knowledge is contextual and fluid.³ Hazle has made a strong argument that the praxis based nature of practical theology has enormous implications for mission and helps us move beyond forms of applied theology:

> Whether the response is personal and corporate, ecclesiastical or political, prophetic or pastoral, theology now seeks to set forth an answer to the question, "what would God have me/us do?" However, and more than that, theology's answer seeks to fulfil, in a given time and context, the ethical demand of God's revelation for that time and place. Theology with a practical paradigm is therefore inescapably missionlogical.⁴

It will require a re-examination of the very word "missional," and perhaps a re-interpretation of it, to arrive at this conclusion—a position that would argue that God is already missionally involved in the concrete, particular, and experiential dimensions of our lives. God's revelation and action, by its very nature, is local and particular. Newbigin defines this as the "scandal of particularity."⁵ Here, the election of Israel in a local cultural context becomes a model (he would probably say more than a model) and endorsement of the gospel coming to life in each local cultural expression.

By claiming that mission, in essence, is local, it could easily be discussed under a subsection of the local dimension of practical theology. This is resisted for several reasons. The first, already mentioned, is a desire to place the missional question in its specific historical context. The fact that this is needed could be demonstrated by attending many evangelically conservative churches today and listening to a sermon. It will soon be discovered that, when many think of the word mission, they equate it with saving souls from an eternity without God. This does not necessarily lead to neglect of other material concerns, but certainly becomes secondary. To correct real imbalances, the correct understanding is essential.

Secondly, I believe it is important to root our reflections in the nature of the triune God. This triune God, by nature is missional, and our mission actually starts with his missional activity.⁶

---

3. Müller, "Transversal Rationality," 5.
4. Hazle, "Practical Theology Today," 349.
5. Newbigin, *The Gospel in a Pluralist Society*, 88.
6. Bosch, *Transforming Mission*, 389–92; Hendriks, *Studying Congregations in Africa*, 25; Van Gelder, *The Ministry of the Missional Church*, 18; Newbigin, *The Open Secret*, 19–29.

Lastly, this missional question is addressed in the belief that it provides a helpful narrative to understand the glocal dimensions of practical theology, as well as questions regarding praxis—so central to a postfoundationalist practical theology. It provides the necessary framework and grounding with which these terms ought to be understood.

The Problem of Missions

The story of mission is as old as Christianity itself. From the very beginning, Paul wrestles with questions of the implication of the life, death, and resurrection of Jesus. The disciples' desire to risk their lives post-Easter (after abandoning Jesus at the cross) in spreading his message of the kingdom all over the known world as Jesus had instructed them, remains one of the great turn-abouts in history. It is the resurrection that gives impetus to this missional activity to which the disciples commit themselves.[7] Of course, for many, the importance of whether they were simply apparitions, or an actual physical resurrection, is beside the point.[8] However, the reality was the explosion of missional activity.

Christian mission in the world has a checkered history, with high points and low points, producing both good and evil. But, as we have noted right from the beginning, there was a commitment to mission, and the Christian faith spread quickly throughout the known world. We are forced to ask the question with one of last century's most famous church historians, "What was this faith which had this remarkable spread?"[9] Was it the intense community life, its new conception of humanity, or both?[10] Whatever the many factors, mission has been at the center of the Christian faith from its inception to the present.

Peter Scott, a missionary to Africa in the nineteenth century, was at the grave of David Livingstone in Westminster Abbey. He looked at his name on the slate and says he had a vision. He saw a line of mission stations passing through East Africa into the "mysteries of the Sahara desert."[11] So began the story of the Africa Inland Mission. What would these mission stations look like? How would they understand the gospel? What do they

---

7. Wright, "The Resurrection," 17.
8. Crossan, "The Resurrection," 46–47.
9. Latourette, *A History*, 45.
10. Stark, *The Rise of Christianity*, 208 and 215.
11. Anderson, *We Felt like Grasshoppers*, 17.

mean by "church"? How would they understand the relationship of Western culture in relation to the indigenous communities?

There has been enough written about the history of mission in South Africa to know exactly what those mission stations looked like and, in fact, still do in certain places. The missionaries' relationship to the colonial authorities remains a fierce debate in many circles. Specifically, within a South African context, Saayman argues that the missions and missionaries were certainly entangled with colonialism and the colonial authorities.[12] He takes an ambivalent position though, arguing that they were simply a product of their times. With the collapse of colonialism, the nature of missions was placed under the spotlight and there was a call for indigenous leadership. There were even calls for a moratorium on missions, which, for long, was not widespread or imposed.[13] The debate was vigorous, but even those, who opted to oppose any form of moratorium, had serious concerns about missions. It was urged that missionaries learn from their mistakes, listen to national voices, and receive training in cross-cultural missions. The call for a moratorium highlighted a real concern to preserve traditional cultures, something that had first gained prominence in Latin America, where the indigenous cultures were collapsing and being exploited.[14]

Despite harsh criticism for the missionaries' role in Africa, others have noted the subversive nature of the very gospel they perpetuated. Lamin Sanneh is one who noted this with regard to the missionaries in their "root conviction that the Gospel is transmissible in the mother tongue, I suggest, missionaries opened the way for the local idiom to gain the ascendancy of foreign superiority."[15]

Sanneh argues that, by adopting the local languages, they extended the principle of Jewish ethnic particularity and, in some ways, helped preserve certain dimensions of local cultures.[16] It is perhaps best to settle on the fact that Western missionaries were a mixed blessing. We should not ignore the real positives, but also own up to their real shortcomings.[17] At this point, it is perhaps pertinent to note the foundationalist danger of an applied theology for a local context. The sense of surety with regard to

12. Saayman, *Christian Mission in South Africa*, 34.
13. Pillay and Hofmeyr, *Perspectives on Church History*, 277.
14. Wakatama, *Independence*, 13.
15. Sanneh, *Encountering the West*, 19.
16. Ibid., 181.
17. Van Der Walt, *Understanding and Rebuilding Africa*, 23–24.

knowledge (whether biblical inerrancy), church tradition, or Western cultural supremacy) caused numerous problems. An affirmation of the local and contextual nature of mission, so central to postfoundationalism, was missing in many cases.

Mission in Historical Perspective

Of course, it is important to note that missions did not start with people being sent to Africa by Western churches. David Bosch's book, *Transforming Missions: Paradigm Shifts in Theology and Mission*, captures the complex development and shifts that took place in mission throughout the ages. Bosch's work has become somewhat of a holy grail in mission studies. It could be fair to say that, for mission studies, it could become what Niebuhr's *Christ and Culture* has been for many in the discussion of the relationship between the church and the world. We cannot hope to capture everything that he says, but will use his work for the express purpose of trying to put mission, and more specifically the missional concept, in its historical frame of reference.

Transforming Mission

Bosch starts by examining the question of mission in the Old Testament, and then moves on into the New Testament. Most people would feel comfortable to note that the modern missionary movement can be evaluated as ambivalent. However, when it comes to the New Testament, a sort of uncritical filter moves over many Christians' eyes as they gaze upon the golden age of Christian mission as the model for all future times. To be honest, with Bosch we must concede that mission in the New Testament was indeed ambivalent.[18] The good, the bad, and the ugly often lay side by side. In his analysis, Bosch examines three missionary paradigms in the New Testament—Matthew, Luke, and Paul. As regards Matthew's paradigm, he argues that one cannot deduce a universally binding missionary theory from it. Despite this, we can look in the same direction as Matthew. Bosch summarizes Matthew's view as follows: "Christians find their true identity when they are involved in mission, in communicating to others a new way of life, a new interpretation of reality and God, and in committing

---

18. Bosch, *Transforming Mission*, 54.

A Postfoundationalist Practical Theology

themselves to the liberation and salvation of others. A missionary community is one that understands itself as being both different from and committed to its environment; it exists within its context in a way which is both winsome and challenging."[19]

In Luke's paradigm, we see a slightly different emphasis than in Matthew. Luke emphasizes the continuing presence of Jesus in the church through the Holy Spirit, who guides the church in mission. This is demonstrated in the correlation between the mission to the Jews and the gentiles. For Luke, great importance is placed on the witness of the church to the events in Jesus's life, which should continue in the church's mission.[20] Great weight is also placed on repentance and forgiveness in turning towards Jesus. However, this should not be interpreted as the saving of souls, which "flatly contradicts Luke's understanding of mission."[21] Luke seems to insist on a new perspective on wealth, which could be seen as the economic justice dimension of mission. It could be argued that this is linked to Luke's belief that Jesus's gospel is one of peace. Peacemaking is central to mission.[22] One of the most important dimensions of Luke's paradigm is the emphasis on the church as a historical manifestation of mission, although notable in its absence of church structure. For Luke, there is also the realization that mission would often encounter adversity and suffering.[23]

When examining Paul's missionary paradigm, Bosch highlights the fact that Paul places great weight on the church as a new community and vanguard of the coming world. In discussing Paul's understanding of mission to the Jews, he treads with great sensitivity without committing himself.[24] Rodney Stark takes quite a radical position on the mission to the Jews believing that large numbers of them were actually converted and that the mission to the Jews was actually quite successful.[25]

Bosch also notes the puzzling nature of Paul's belief in the imminent triumph of God—one which is hard to resolve, but should still remain central for mission. With regard to involvement in society, Bosch concludes that Paul encouraged participation in society but, at other times,

19. Ibid., 83.
20. Ibid.,114, 115, and 116.
21. Ibid.,117.
22. Ibid.,118.
23. Ibid.,120 and 121.
24. Bosch, *Transforming Mission*, 172 and 174.
25. Stark, *The Rise of Christianity*, 69–70.

discouraged it. This remains a hot topic of debate. What is not a hot topic of debate is that much of Paul's mission took place with much difficulty and personal weakness, and that his aim was the proclamation of Jesus's message and the reality of unconditional love and unmerited grace.[26]

Bosch concludes his examination of the New Testament by noting that we cannot simply jump from a discussion of the church's primitive mission to the present-day situation, without paying attention to mission within the church's history.[27] He begins by looking at the Eastern church's missionary paradigm, which was significantly different from that of primitive Christianity. It worked out theology from the bottom up in order to make sense to the Greek mind.[28] There was also a universalizing tendency toward a Hellenization of the faith, yet without departing from the essentials of the Christian faith by "affirming the Old Testament, the historicity of the humanity of Jesus, [and] the bodily resurrection of Jesus from the dead."[29]

The other dimension of the Eastern paradigm was the monastic movement that spread widely throughout Christianity, which ought to be considered a form of mission—and indeed was quite successful.[30] The significant weakness of this model is that it tends to synchronize religion with society, which then moves beyond inculturation and contextualization. It often assimilates in too radical a manner with the existing political setup and can end up being overly nationalistic. It can also be in-grown and pay little attention to those who do not agree with its doctrinal formulations.[31] Perhaps, the most striking loss with regard to the primitive dimension of mission was the loss of eschatology, rooted in the promise of Christ to intervene in this world. It moved to a salvation that was totally concerned with another world, and the attempt to move towards that and "even when believers do get involved in the contingencies of historical life, they do so with reservations and often with a bad conscience."[32]

The second paradigm that Bosch examines is the medieval Roman Catholic paradigm. This is the period roughly from 600 CE to 1500 CE, which was dominated by a belief that the pagans and those outside the

---

26. Bosch, *Transforming Mission*, 174–78.
27. Ibid., 189.
28. Ibid., 211.
29. Ibid.
30. Ibid., 212.
31. Ibid.
32. Ibid., 213.

church ought to be compelled to enter into the church—if necessary by force.[33] Now, the church was a large organization whose connections with Judaism were severed. Despite the often accompanying negative assessment with regard to a discussion of Constantine, we must acknowledge that it could have been no other way and that we would have done the same.[34] By far, the most damaging impact on mission in this paradigm was the individualization of salvation with its roots in Augustine and his battle with Pelagius.[35] Augustine's clash with the Donatists defined the ecclesialization of salvation, where salvation could not be found outside commitment and participation in the church.[36] Before it seems that Bosch is on an Augustinian bashing session, he qualifies his critique: "Given the historical alternatives he and others had before them, they were the only choices that made sense to them. And it is appropriate to ask whether our choices, in similar circumstances, would have been any better, even if they were different."[37]

The third paradigm for missions is that of the Protestant Reformation. Bosch notes that the Protestant emphasis on God's sovereignty often paralyzed the missionary movement while, at other times, was held in tension with human accountability. This polar tension was demonstrated further in the reality that people were often seen exclusively as sinners while, at other times, Christ's love for humans was emphasized. This tension was further expressed in the objective and subjective dimensions of faith.[38] The relation between church and state was close, and had an enormous influence on mission (the Anabaptists being the exception).

Following the Protestant Reformation, Bosch deals with mission in the wake of the Enlightenment. His extensive treatment of this era culminates in stating the complex, varied, oppositional, polemical nature of its various dimensions. Bosch comments, "There was virtually no trace of a unified pattern of thought and practice. Sometimes Christians responded in widely divergent ways to the challenge posed to the Christian mission by the Enlightenment."[39]

33. Ibid., 236.
34. Ibid., 237.
35. Ibid., 215.
36. Ibid., 218.
37. Ibid., 222.
38. Ibid., 261.
39. Ibid., 342.

Bosch discusses the motifs and motives that emerged within the Enlightenment paradigm. The subject-object dichotomy found expression in both liberal and conservative approaches to the Bible. Regardless of this approach, there still was in both (liberal and conservative) a tendency to treat those in other cultures as objects, rather than as one of their own. The belief that mission would indeed be successful was seen as possible only if the right conditions were set up with regard to social progress. Or alternatively, if people were converted, this would lead to social betterment.[40] Missionaries believed that progress was indeed possible, even inevitable, as Western culture made itself known and continued to spread. For the liberals, this progress was often seen as the goal of the gospel, and thus had a *this-worldly* focus. On the other hand, focusing on the salvation of souls resulted in an *otherworldly* focus.[41] This belief that things were solvable led to a vast explosion in mission agencies and volunteers.

Perhaps the saddest divide to emerge during this period was the God-human divide: "If the aim of mission was viewed as giving glory to God, this was interpreted as slighting the value and contribution of humans; if the inherent capability of human beings to make the right choices and act ethically was emphasized, this was seen as a refusal to give all credit to God."[42] The shadow of the Enlightenment loomed large over missionaries of all kinds. Although a sense of tolerance emerged, and a somewhat relativistic perspective, a Western sense of superiority and prejudice was common. We must also not be too quick to blame the missionaries of this period, as they brought the gospel as they knew it, despite the negative consequences and superiority that accompanied it.[43]

Bosch believes that, in the area of missions a real shift is taking place, to which he refers as the *postmodern paradigm*. The collapse of foundationalist rationalism as an Enlightenment bastion, and one that can solve all of the world's problems is a growing reality, as noted. This does not lead to a total rejection of rationality, but rather to what Stanley Grenz refers as a *chastened rationality*. This again demonstrates the importance of critical realism as a middle way that van Huyssteen reminds us of, affirming the contextual and fallibilist nature of our knowledge, yet affirming that things can be known.

40. Ibid.
41. Ibid., 343.
42. Ibid.
43. Ibid., 344.

A Postfoundationalist Practical Theology

This will possibly allow for a greater role of religion within society, but one which will be "chastened and humble,"[44] consistent with postfoundationalism. Bosch argues that there is a definite move beyond the subject-object scheme of the Enlightenment. This has resulted in a missiology that does not allow any object (whether human or nature) to be subject to the chains of rationality, as objects to be manipulated and exploited by others.[45] The belief that the world is not shaped by a set of unchangeable laws that contain humanity and society has led to the belief in hopeful change for many people. This hope also is a chastened one, which does not accept that all progress is good and inevitable. In terms of mission, this would bring into question notions of development (whether technological, social or personal), which often are seen as the result of the Christian message.[46] This chastened postfoundational optimism, together with the other changes mentioned, leads towards a greater interdependence with others and a turn away from individualistic and monolithic conceptions of the world.[47] Paul Hiebert attempts to capture some of these missiological implications in light of this shift away from the Enlightenment by noting:

> In a postmodern world we need to re-examine our epistemological foundations to see how they affect our relationships to other people, cultures, theologies, and religions in a pluralistic world. I am convinced that critical realism is a biblical approach to knowledge. I am also convinced it is the approach we must take in a post-colonial era in missions. We must deal with cultural, religious, and theological pluralism with deep conviction about the truth, but without arrogance and paternalism.[48]

Earlier, we have already engaged with this postmodern paradigm. Postmodernism's attack on Enlightenment's foundationalist assumptions has helped us to move into a postfoundational space. Hiebert's quote, like van Huyssteen has suggested, argues that a critical realist approach helps us to move in this direction.

Taking further the discussion regarding the postmodern paradigm, Bosch sets out to describe what he believes to be the emerging missionary

---

44. Ibid., 355.
45. Ibid.
46. Ibid., 358.
47. Ibid., 362.
48. Hiebert, *Anthropological Reflections*, 51.

paradigm today. Here, some of his material and insights will be used, but under headings directly relevant to our present discussion.

Missional Salvation and Practical Theology

Today, the question of salvation—what it means and its implications—is part of the emerging missional paradigm. We believe that a missional practical theology ought to have a specific view of mission that takes these developments into account. A discussion of missional salvation will combine the concerns that Bosch raises under his various sections on mission—as mediating salvation, justice, evangelism, liberation, action in hope and interaction with other faiths.

The question of salvation is complex. As seen in the various paradigms with which Bosch has worked, there was a move toward a salvation located in the church. There was also an individualization of salvation in the Eastern Orthodox, Protestant, and Enlightenment paradigms. A greater awareness of the social dimension of the gospel was also seen to emerge in the Enlightenment, albeit with a superiority complex. Within the postmodern paradigm, a greater humility in interacting with other religions and a chastened approach to development was seen. The postmodern or post-colonial realities, and the rejection of exploitative authority, are evident in the various quests for liberation from oppression.

There are various dimensions that need to be considered when engaging with the question of salvation. These questions involve aspects of kingdom versus church, and personal salvation versus social concern. There is a significant overlap within these two poles, but both seem to engage with concerns that a missional practical theology ought to consider.

Kingdom versus Church

Here, the specific focus is to examine whether the location of God's action is in the church and its role in the world, or whether the locus of God's action is in the world primarily—or a combination of both. Practical theology as we have seen has come to affirm that God is active in all dimensions of life and sought to explore what shape that takes. Further, if all dimensions of life are under the missional focus of the triune God, then it follows that a correlational hermeneutic must be affirmed. Different branches of

A Postfoundationalist Practical Theology

knowledge are all in the business of discovering where God is at work. It is not just in the realm of the traditional theological disciplines.

I however, do not want to create false dichotomies, but to highlight simply that one's focus in terms of either kingdom or church has significant consequences for practical theology. If the church is seen to be equated with an extension of God's kingdom, or even as God's kingdom, we are left with a negative view toward the culture and lives of which we are part. Here, membership of the church becomes all important, and participation in the world and culture secondary, in that participation in this world is tolerated as a way of bringing people into the church (hence God's kingdom), or using the resources of culture and the world to extend God's growth through growing the church. This emphasis on the church leads quite naturally to the propagation of other-worldly salvation (as opposed to a worldly, or cosmic one), as well as a quest for *winning souls* (as opposed to a holistic salvation). These other two concerns will be addressed later.

We can see that these complementary concerns expressed clearly when church growth becomes the goal of mission, and the concerns of the world are regarded as periphery. Donald McGavran's book, *Understanding Church Growth*, is just such an example of this approach. At the time it set in motion a church growth movement that has flourished in many quarters around the world. More importantly, it espouses the view that evangelicals and many others have internalized, and continue to propagate. The following quote from McGavran illustrates this:

> The chief and irreplaceable purpose of mission is church growth. Social services please God, but it must never be substituted for finding the lost. Our Lord did not rest content with feeding the hungry and healing the sick. He pressed on to give his life as a ransom for many and to send out his followers to disciple all nations. Service must not be so disproportionately emphasized at the expense of evangelism that findable persons are continually lost. In the proportioning of social ministries and church planting, the degree of growth being achieved must always be taken into account.[49]

Later, McGavran goes on to state that the supreme task ahead is the multiplication of churches.[50] This view was also evident in the British context in the work of the late David Watson.[51] Although hesitant to equate the church

---

49. MacGavran, *Understanding Church Growth*, 22.
50. Ibid., 31.
51. Watson, *I Believe in the Church*, 51.

Postfoundationalist Reflections in Practical Theology

with the kingdom, he stills sees the spread of the church, with conversions of individuals, as tied to the spread of the kingdom of God.[52] His whole discussion regarding the kingdom always begins with, or returns to, questions regarding the church and her role in the world.[53] Many will note that the two examples used here come from within the evangelical tradition. Of course, one can see this demonstrated in other segments of Christianity, yet it remains a unique evangelical problem where evangelism (they have resisted the word mission) is seen as *church extension*.[54] However, there are radical evangelicals who are aware of just such a problem. Ballard and Pritchard mention one of these, Chris Sudgen, in his analysis of the praxis model.[55] Sudgen comments that, very early on, many came to believe that "the kingdom of God was a matter of faith that had nothing to do with society. They believed that God's activity and kingdom were locked into the church."[56] This focus on the church often leads to embracing a status-quo approach with regard to political and social realities. Somehow, it claims neutrality with regard to the world. In the political arena, its focus on church life can lead to a disengagement from political issues, endorsing the status quo, and refusing to be aware of one's own political assumptions.[57]

Essentially, what we have been discussing is a fusion between the kingdom and the church, which sees the kingdom of God, at least in its temporal earthly dimensions, as synonymous with the extension of his church throughout the world. On the other side of the coin is the reality that often the world outside the church is viewed as the kingdom of God itself. This, of course, has its roots in early times with the conversion of Constantine and the complex interrelationship between the church and the state that followed—referred to as the *Christendom model*. The desire for the perfect Christian society, also known as *Corpus Christianum*, attained its climax under Innocent III just prior to the birth of Thomas Aquinas.[58]

Alan Hirsch attempts to describe this phenomenon, which is Christendom:

---

52. Ibid., 54–56.
53. Ibid., 51–63.
54. Bosch, *Transforming Mission*, 415.
55. Ballard and Pritchard, *Practical Theology in Action*, 73.
56. Samuel and Sugden, "God's Intention for the World," 150.
57. Saayman, *Christian Mission in South Africa*, 11.
58. Latourette, *A History*, 514.

A Postfoundationalist Practical Theology

> Christendom is the name given to the sacral culture that has dominated European society from around the eleventh century until the end of the twentieth. Its sources go back to the time when Constantine came to the throne of the Roman Empire and granted Christians complete freedom of worship and even favoured Christianity; thereby undermining all other religions in the empire.[59]

Of course, the church did not always dominate the state; in fact, it was most often the reverse. This, despite the attempts of the papacy to invoke the forged Donation of Constantine, claimed to be written by Constantine to the then pope, Silvester I. This purported to give the church and the pope authority over the empire.[60] Shenk, who places the roots of Christendom in the fourth century, notes that the consequences of equating society with the church leads to the collapse of any sense of mission.[61] Mission tends to advance by force, which is what Bosch notes with regard to some forms of the Roman Catholic paradigm in mission. This collusion between society and church, and its eventual demise under the weight of secularism, lead to a crisis in mission and a crisis for the church. The most obvious response was the shift to equate the kingdom with the church, in the sense of the churches' growth and the individual's salvation. However, the approach that seeks for a partnering of church and state is not something that has "left the building" with the rise of secularism. Islam does not consider state affairs to be a distraction from spirituality, "but is the stuff of religion itself."[62] In modern-day America, we have witnessed the attempt by certain Christian groups to win back the government, and hence society as just such a modern manifestation of what we are talking about.[63] Here, the danger lies in the two extremes. On the one hand, swallowing up the kingdom into the church and, on the other hand, swallowing up the church into the kingdom. The swallowing up of the church into the kingdom poses huge problems. Bosch notes that in the 1960s, with Hoekendijk and others at the Strasbourg Conference, "the idea of the world providing the agenda for the church and the church having to identify completely with this agenda first

---

59. Frost and Hirsch, *The Shaping of Things to Come*, 8.
60. Southern, *Western Society and the Church*, 91.
61. Shenk, *Write the Vision*, 35.
62. Armstrong, *Islam*, xi.
63. Castells, *The Information Age*, 29.

surfaced clearly." In this scenario, the church became overtaxed, and any distinction between world and church disappeared completely.[64]

The question then becomes, in what manner will the church relate to the world, and how should the kingdom and the church be seen? A fuller discussion of this will take place with regard to the church's role, when we explore the missional nature of the church. At this point, I merely wish to point out that the church is simply not the kingdom. The kingdom is broader than the church and includes all of life. God's kingdom is manifested in the smallest atoms and particles here on earth to the furthest cosmic realities with its planets and galaxies. It involves the most destitute dimensions of human life and our highest achievements and goals. It is an all-of-life reality. If the church were to cease to exist, God would still be manifest in his world. It is obvious that the argument here is for a balance between transcendence and immanence. In saying this, the argument would also be that the church is one of God's primary vehicles to testify to the arrival of his kingdom, in the now, but also in the not-yet. The not-yet dimension helps one to guard against the excessive optimism of the Enlightenment paradigm in missions, as well as to guard against the utopian idea of a Christian society or kingdom. Therefore, the church is a body of people who are dedicated to God's dream for the world (his kingdom) and seek to embody it in their relations, not only with themselves but with the whole of his kingdom. It encourages its members to participate in this dream. But, at the same time, it makes common cause and calls others, who are not its members, to participate in God's kingdom project. It believes, like Cornelius in the book of Acts, that the prayers and good deeds, which arise from those who are not Christians, are a sweet-smelling incense to God. It affirms that, often, those outside the church are better at extending God's rule and reign on the earth than those inside the church. People can participate in the kingdom without knowing the King. The church then ought to call those participants into relationship with the One they are already serving. Sometimes, the church (not necessarily the church corporate, but the individual members) will be driven by the concerns of the world and yet, at other times, not. The tension between nature and grace, kingdom and church, immanence and transcendence, will often require a prophetic stance as one stands against some of the world's programs. This discernment is no easy task. As will be mentioned later, practical theology is therefore obliged to, and in fact mostly does, see the whole of the earth

---

64. Bosch, *Transforming Mission*, 382–84.

A Postfoundationalist Practical Theology

as a concern and locus for reflection and action, not just the components of church life. It also must acknowledge that the starting point can be in the very real daily concerns of humankind, as they have within them elements of God's revelation and concern. This again affirms the importance of the local in a postfoundationalist approach. A practical theology that holds the church and kingdom in creative tension must now answer the question as to the nature of salvation.

Personal Salvation and Cosmic Redemption

In what follows, it will be argued that salvation is not simply restricted to the personal domain of our lives. Bosch calls such a position—that locates salvation in the individual—as untenable and a manifestation of the Enlightenment paradigm.[65] God seeks to bring cosmic salvation and redemption to our world, not just to individuals. McLaren asks the question, what would it be like if Jesus's message was not just about personal salvation, but had

> practical implications for such issues as how you lived your daily life, how you earn and spend money, how you treat people of other races and religions, and how the nations of the world conduct their foreign policy? What if his message directly or indirectly addressed issues like, advertising, environmentalism, terrorism, economics, sexuality, marriage, parenting, the quest for happiness and peace, and racial reconciliation?[66]

Although McLaren captures something of what a move beyond a personal salvation paradigm should look like, it is Newbigin's words that we believe best illustrates this. He states that the gospel is "good news about God's universal reign. It is directed to the whole of human and cosmic reality,"[67] and believes that the perspective of the Bible indicates just such a universalistic overtone, bringing all of history and the cosmos under God's redemptive purposes.[68]

The focus on the personal dimension of salvation often takes on quite a specific bent with regard to the need for a personal and individual

---

65. Ibid., 397.
66. McLaren, *The Secret Message of Jesus*, 4.
67. Newbigin, *The Open Secret*, 66.
68. Ibid., 78.

conversion. It is argued that, one day, God will destroy the earth and create a new heaven and a new earth. Therefore, the need to participate in making this world a better place is seen as counter productive. This form of understanding the world is often linked to forms of evangelicalism that adhere to a pre-millenialist view with regard to eschatology.[69] Bosch argues that our eschatology under the emerging missionary paradigm must allow for a tension between our participation and God's final consummation of the world.[70] Within American evangelical circles, Ladd was someone who was instrumental in bringing a balance between pre- and post-millennial camps. He argues that biblical eschatology, and the tension that Bosch describes, is that of a now-not-yet reality.[71]

The focus on the personal dimension of salvation, at the expense of engaging salvation in a broader sense, has its roots in the notion that humans are destined for an eternity in hell. The leading evangelical conservative today explains his view of salvation:

> When Adam and Eve sinned, they became worthy of eternal punishment and separation from God (Gen 2:17). In the same way, when human beings sin today they become liable to the wrath of God and to eternal punishment: "The wages of sin is death" (Rom 6:23). This means that once people sin, God's justice could require only one thing—that they be eternally separated from God, cut off from experiencing any good from him, and that they live forever in hell, receiving only wrath eternally.[72]

This view is seen as central in mission. Conservative commentators have argued that the attack on the doctrine of hell is one of the greatest threats today from mission. They argue that it makes mission impotent and unwarranted. The researcher finds it quite ironic that many who see the rejection of eternal damnation as a rejection of mission, also hold to a strict predestination that should lead to the same rejection of mission, if they are consistent.[73] Despite the fact that this view can paralyze mission, as Walls and Dongell note, it often has the reverse effect, whereby those who believe they are elected feel that they cannot remain inactive and therefore have to

---

69. Grenz and Olson, *Twentieth Century Theology*, 146–47.
70. Bosch, *Transforming Mission*, 510.
71. Ladd, *A Theology of the New Testament*, 210.
72. Grudem, *Systematic Theology*, 657.
73. Walls and Dongell, *Why I Am Not a Calvinist*, 196–97.

A Postfoundationalist Practical Theology

participate in mission.[74] It is also the case with those who believe that the end of the world is near are driven to great sacrifice to save as many people as possible.

However, when one moves beyond a narrow view of salvation, to a broader and more cosmic view, your picture of God and that of the world around you changes. De Gruchy believes judgement to be an important concept, but demonstrates the crassness of the doctrine of hell and its absurdity:

> To believe that God has devised and maintained a prison torture chamber infinite in extent and reminiscent of the worst concentration camp for those who step out of line demeans God and destroys the integrity of the gospel. Can the God revealed in Jesus Christ, and those who have spent their lives trying to "save the lost", be "eternally blest" while those they failed to convert are being tormented eternally in hell? The idea is bizarre. It is even more theologically obscene to think that a believing Christian who is the commandant of a concentration camp will go to heaven, and those Jews, gypsies and homosexuals whom he incarcerated and killed will end up in Hell. Is Ghandi, a Hindu, to be excluded, and a member of the Klu Klux Klan who, in the name of a "white Christ," bombed a black church, killing children, to be welcomed by St. Peter with open arms?[75]

More moderate evangelicals caution us against this received doctrine of hell and note that the end time is one of surprises,[76] and that we should not speculate on who is in or who is out. On the other hand, it probably is important to note that Jesus's comments around hell are more about the judgement in this present world against a rebellious Israel, rather than an other-worldly reality.

It might seem strange to enter into a discussion of hell in a paper on practical theology! However, it is our contention that the doctrine is so pervasive in Christian circles that it is woven into the very fabric of the non-reflective theology of many and their "theory laden practice."[77] Its deep roots continue to push Christians to other-worldly concerns at the expense of engaging in a broader program of salvation. It provides a warped and one-sided view of mission. A missional practical theology will need to address

74. Bosch, *Transforming Mission*, 258.
75. De Gruchy, *Being Human*, 155–56.
76. Grenz, *Renewing the Center*, 286.
77. Browning, *A Fundamental Practical Theology*, 47.

this doctrine of hell, and communicate a reworked critical understanding of it, which can be available to the masses. This becomes important as the discipline begins to engage more directly with the evangelical world.

The work of Brian McLaren is just one such attempt to wrestle with this issue. His book, *The Last Word and the Word after That,* is a popular attempt at this. McLaren believes that Jesus threatened people with inclusion, not exclusion.[78] Of course, in certain Christian sectors, McLaren's view has not been received well at all.[79] The recent firestorm over Rob Bell's book, *Love Wins,* has shown how sensitive a topic this is.

So, what do we speak of when we think of a broad view of salvation? Brian McLaren refers to it as "God's dream for the world." Marcus Borg refers to it differently as the "dream of God."[80] For me, this thought has taken root and captures the cosmic nature of redemption—the sense that all of life is charged with God's presence and, in fact, is a sacrament. It is a place where God's presence can be encountered and embraced. One's work and play are encounters with the most high God. This is despite the fact that the world remains deeply scarred. The person who enjoyed the sunset at the ocean the night before the tsunami struck in South-East Asia would have marveled at the beauty of our world. The same person would have come face to face with the deep contradiction that is our world's burden when, the next day, a giant wave rose up to wreak havoc and death. More examples can be given, not only from nature, but from one's own personal and existential struggles. Paul Tillich notes that, at our very core, we are anxious beings. We are anxious because of the awareness that death awaits all of us. It requires great courage, the courage to be, in the face of this threat of non-being.

> It is not the realization of universal transitoriness, not even the experience of the death of others, but the impression of these events on the always latent awareness of our own having to die, that produces anxiety. Anxiety is finitude, experienced as one's own finitude. This is the natural anxiety of man as man, and in some way of all living beings. It is the anxiety of non-being, the awareness of one's finitude as finitude.[81]

---

78. McLaren, *The Last Word,* 247.
79. Carson, *Becoming Conversant,* 168–69.
80. Borg, *The God We Never Knew,* 132.
81. Tillich, *The Courage to Be,* 44.

A Postfoundationalist Practical Theology

What we as Christians admit is, both the beauty and ugliness that characterize both the bacteria (pro-biotics) that heals us, as well as the virus that kills us. We realize both the reality of Tutu's work for peace and, in contradistinction, Hitler's work for destruction. We are aware of the sunsets and the tsunamis. However, we affirm that this does not remain God's dream for the world, and that we have been promised a picture of hope that gives us the courage to be. Therefore, we believe that God will intervene in the future and partner with humanity in the creation of God's good world. In the light of this, the good we do and contribute towards in this world, carries on into the next, and indeed we are rewarded for our good works.

What does this broad view of salvation mean for practical theology? It means that a cure for HIV/AIDS is a direct concern for practical theology, as well as the care and provision for its victims. Any future settlement on Mars, and how it is conducted, would be a concern for practical theology, as much as the worship of a small church in the Karoo. The current virtues and vices of globalization are the domain of practical theology, as well as the concerns of biology and ethics. All these areas are charged with God's presence, and he is there. In the daily experiences of humanity, the flow of the Spirit can be detected and tentatively uncovered. God has a dream.[82] With deep humility and weakness, as with the cross, we seek to embrace God's dream, and the whole broad salvation he brings to the world in light of his resurrection. Practical theology is a practical theology of hope. It believes the best about our world and sees its entirety as the locus of its focus. What can this hope look like? This section concludes with the words of Moltmann who attempts to paint its contours:

> Hence all its knowledge will be an anticipatory, fragmentary knowledge forming a prelude to the promised future, and as such is committed to hope. Hence also vice versa the hope which arises from faith in God's promise will become the ferment in our thinking, its mainspring, the source of its restlessness and torment. The hope that it is continually led on further by the promise of God reveals all thinking in history to be eschatologically orientated and eschatologically stamped as provisional. If hope draws faith into the realm of thought and life, then it can no longer consider itself to be an eschatological hope as distinct from the minor hopes that are directed towards attainable goals and visible changes in human life, neither can it as a result disassociate itself from such hopes by relegating them to a different sphere while considering its own

82. Borg, *The God We Never Knew*, 133.

future to be supra-wordly and purely spiritual in character. The Christian hope is directed towards a *novum ultimum*, towards a new creation of all things by the God of the resurrection of Jesus Christ.[83]

Trinitarian Mission and Practical Theology

If the modern missionary pattern is broader than a personal salvation, and mission involves the creative tension between the church and the kingdom, so it ought to be with practical theology, which is missional in its commitment to all of life. All dimensions of our lives, therefore, fall under the orbit of its reflection and study. Practical theology is missional in the sense that it is a witness to, and a commitment to, God's dream for the world.[84] In this dream, it must participate through reflection and practice in a holistic and broad manner. But why be missional in the first place? Why concern oneself at all with questions around God's kingdom and cosmic plan? The answer to these questions is that, at the very center of our faith, in the very being and heart of God, is the desire for mission. The triune God is in the business of putting the world right. We are on a mission because God is on a mission.

Before exploring the triune God as missional, two criticisms must be addressed. The first is the criticism as to why traditional doctrinal formulations should form any part of practical theology. The second, being linked to the first, is the question as to how we can know anything about God at all. The second criticism is perhaps easier to address than the first. No attempt will be made to give a thorough response to either, but, rather, why both are regarded as important will be highlighted.

The Trinity in Practical Theology?

A missional practical theology embraces the reality and usefulness of a Trinitarian formula, as it is one of the central aspects of our faith. The Trinity is a belief that is accepted by all forms of Christianity across the great traditions—Catholic, Protestant and Orthodox, Reformed, Pentecostal and Charismatic. The twentieth century has witnessed a bourgeoning interest

---

83. Moltmann, *Theology of Hope*, 33.
84. Borg, *The God We Never Knew*, 133.

A Postfoundationalist Practical Theology

in the doctrine of the Trinity, as Stanley Grenz's book, *Rediscovering the Triune God*, demonstrates. In this regard, he notes:

> Far from being a secret, the doctrine of the Trinity has become one of the most widely acknowledged Christian teachings, exploring the triunity of God has developed into one of the most popular theological pursuits, and Trinitarian theology has emerged as one of the most widely touted theological labels, encompassing the efforts of thinkers representing nearly every ecclesiological tradition and theological persuasion.[85]

Alongside this widespread agreement about the importance of the Trinity, is the acknowledgment that practical theology is theological, after all. Part of what this means is that it takes the Bible and Christian tradition seriously. It believes that, although God reveals himself in various ways in experience, culture, and reason, he has revealed himself in the events recorded in the Bible and throughout Christian history (despite its flaws and human frailty). Ward has lamented the fact that practical theology is so fearful of doctrine, or specifically theological statements.[86] We need to move beyond this fear.

Therefore, from a theological and a Christian point of view, questions around the Trinity and God's nature can provide a useful perspective in understanding mission, and the missional task of practical theology. Koopman has argued for the importance of the Trinity for forms of public theology strongly, noting that:

> This triune work establishes, confirms and actualises the dignity and worth of all humans and of the rest of creation. God's love for the world, which comes to expression in the magnalia Dei, does have meaning, significance, and implications for all dimensions and terrains of life, from the most private, personal, and intimate to the most public, open, social, and cosmic. At its heart, therefore, Christian theology is public theology. It reflects on the love of the God who is at work in all spheres of life. Moreover, the caring, liberating and renewing work of the triune God does have dignifying implications for the whole of creation, for all of reality. It may be helpful to identify three basic questions.[87]

---

85. Grenz, *Rediscovering the Triune God*, 1.
86. Ward, "The Hermeneutical," 58, 60.
87. Koopman, "Some Contours," 123–24.

These considerations, of course, might lead naturally to the rebuttal that this theology is from above and given to abstract theory and philosophical speculation. The counter to this assertion is that all experience and culture, in fact, are theory laden from the start. In avoiding this danger, it is also important that we allow for our view of the Trinity to be open to critical reflection and re-appraisal from culture and experience. Of course, some might feel that this opens us up to the charge of relativity.

The practical consequences of a correct understanding of the doctrine of the Trinity can be amply demonstrated in the current "war" in evangelical circles regarding the role of women in the home and in ministry. A hierarchical view of the Trinity results in Bruce Ware (past president of the Evangelical Theological Society in America) noting that the female actually participates in the image of God through reliance upon the male, "particularly manifest in the home and community of faith."[88] On the other hand, an egalitarian perspective on the Trinity leads to a more open view with regard to women, as Kevin Giles notes when he comments: "The doctrine of the Trinity categorically and unambiguously rejects the eternal subordination of the Son and the Spirit in being and work, it does not and cannot be used to support the subordination of women to men, nor to demonstrate that personal equality can be reconciled with permanent subordination."[89] Therefore, in light of the fact of the doctrine of the Trinity's centrality as part of faith and scholarship, it is incumbent upon practical theology to attend to it. However, it must not get locked up in an overtly doctrinal perspective, but allow for revision and correction.

Knowledge of God's Being?

The question regarding the nature of the Trinity leads to the addressing of the second concern that one might have with regard to the importance of Trinitarian thought for practical theology. This is the question of how we can know anything about God at all. Again, according to Hastings, practical theology has had a resistance to making "positive theological statements about the agency of God."[90] A critical realist approach helps us make these statements in the balanced manner we ought, consistent with a postfoundationalist approach.

88. Ware, "Male and Female Complementarity," 92.
89. Giles, "The Subordination," 352.
90. Hastings, *Practical Theology*, 8.

A Postfoundationalist Practical Theology

I realize that, in some senses, it is true that any ontological statement regarding the nature of God and the Trinity must come in the wrapping of anthropological language. We must also acknowledge that we can only know things about God in the events in which he has chosen to reveal himself along with our error-ridden attempts to record and reflect upon these events. In this sense, our understanding of the Trinity, imparted to us through the Scriptures and tradition, arises out of our experience of God and our cultural tools used to express that experience. This is demonstrated in the very terminology of the Father and Son with its patriarchal overtones, as well as the Greek philosophical concepts that the early councils chose to understand about the relationships within the Godhead. We have to acknowledge that our statements about God's nature and reality are second-order theological statements we affirm by faith, with the aid of reason. How faithful our reasoning is, however, is open to debate and critique. In his book on Pannenberg, entitled *Reason for Hope*, Stanley Grenz believes Pannenberg's understanding of the Trinity and God arises out of God's activity in history.[91] However, even Pannenberg[92] would argue that, where one's traditional understanding of God cannot absorb changed experiences taking place in the world, it "must make room for a new experience of God more capable of fulfilling this task." Pannenberg believes that, if we can know anything of the Trinity and God in the Bible revealed in historical events, it has to be an indirect revelation.[93] Louw is one who rejects any form of ontological speculation that arises out of an analysis of our cultural and social existence.[94] We are aware of the strength of this position and therefore admit to the metaphorical and symbolic nature of our pronouncements, which remain an *attempt* to get to grips with the God-human encounter in history.[95]

Despite these difficulties and taking these considerations into account, a venture will be proposed that the God revealed in history has revealed himself as a Trinity. This cannot be proven conclusively, and must be open to revision and further revelation. This further revelation lies at the consummation of history as presently lived.

---

91. Grenz, *Reason for Hope*, 70.
92. Pannenberg, *The Apostles' Creed*, 25.
93. Dulles, "Pannenberg on Revelation and Faith," 171.
94. Louw, *A Pastoral Hermeneutic*, 82.
95. Ibid., 83.

Postfoundationalist Reflections in Practical Theology

Taking these presuppositions into account, it will now be argued that God is missional in his triune nature. I believe that this God is still presently *in mission* outside of our participation, alongside our participation, and with our participation. A missional practical theology acknowledges the Triune God's presence in culture and experience, in the *stuff* of our world. A postfoundationalist approach to practical theology, which takes seriously the local and contextual aspects, finds itself at the coalface of the Triune God's very mission on this earth. And, because this mission is broad, a postfoundationalist approach to practical theology that is local and contextual, will unearth God's very activity and interest in all dimensions of life. We further participate in this mission because God is missional by nature and is presently in mission ahead of us. Affirming this, we must now ask ourselves: What is this mission of God, or, what has come to be known as the *missio Dei*?

The Missio Dei

In our historical sketch, we noted Bosch's comment that mission has often been seen through the lens of personal salvation, church expansion or, alternatively, understood in cultural terms. All these aspects tend to place our efforts at the center. However, in recent times, there has been a decisive shift toward understanding mission as God's mission.[96] Bosch comments that, in fact, it was Barth who first gave impetus to the idea that mission was to be derived from God's nature.[97] Today, it is important that we now see mission as an extension of God's very being.[98] Mission is firstly God's mission and is broad in scope.

> Since God's concern is for the entire world, this should also be the scope of the *missio Dei*. It affects all people in all aspects of their existence. Mission is God's turning to the world in respect of creation, care, redemption and consummation. . . . The *missio Dei* is God's activity which embraces both the church and the world, and in which the church may be privileged to participate.[99]

---

96. Bosch, *Transforming Mission*, 389.
97. Ibid., 390.
98. Hendriks, *Studying Congregations in Africa*, 25.
99. Bosch, *Transforming Mission*, 391.

Missionary activity, therefore, encounters a God who has secretly been at work.[100] We noted earlier with Hoekendijk how often the expanding of the term "mission" led almost to an exclusion of the church, and the swallowing up of the church in the world. Despite these over-corrections, mission ought still to be seen in the width with which Bosch has described it. Its source though remains God's being and heart: "Mission has its origin in the heart of God. God is a fountain of sending love. This is the deepest source of mission. It is impossible to penetrate deeper still; there is mission because God loves people."[101]

Graham et al. note with interest how the Trinity influences those within the emergent church, and others in their corporate theological reflection with regard to mission.[102] Root has argued for the importance of a Trinitarian understanding for practical theology and highlights the incarnation as central for leading us deep into the human situation.[103] With the risk of overstating the obvious, this is a vital dimension of a postfoundationalist perspective. In light of this renewed emphasis of a missional Triune God, we need to ask how we can understand this Trinitarian mission. In what way do the Father, Son, and Spirit participate in, and embody, the mission of God? One of the ways people have chosen to understand the Triune God as missional is by seeing the three persons of the Trinity in terms of certain roles—creator, redeemer, and sanctifier. We shall be using Leslie Newbigin's Trinitarian missiology to help us with this, but must first make a few comments regarding the gender of the Trinity. In today's world, we cannot simply speak of Father and Son without some form of explanation. A quote by Hans Küng has been chosen to illustrate the perspective to which we hold:

> that God is not male, that God is neither masculine nor feminine, that God transcends masculinity and femininity, that all our terms for God, including the word "Father," are only analogies and metaphors, only symbols and ciphers, and that none "fixes" the symbol God, so that one might, say, obstruct women's liberation in society and the ordination of women in the church in the name of such a patriarchal God.[104]

---

100. Ibid.
101. Ibid., 392.
102. Graham et al., *Theological Reflection*, 132.
103. Root, "Practical Theology," 54, 63.
104. Küng, *Credo*, 29.

Louw shows the power of God-images in people's lives. He challenges us to uncover the patriarchal dimensions of our view of God. He also speaks of how the term "fatherhood" (or motherhood for that matter) could provoke negativity for many. He proposes an understanding of God as soul friend.[105] Taking these considerations into account here, a choice will still be made to work with the terms "Father" and "Son," noting their metaphorical nature and how they have arisen out of a patriarchal context. Would a better term perhaps be the "parental nature of mission"?

Newbigin believes that our understanding of the Trinity arises from the axioms of our culture, from the authority of revelation, and can provide practical wisdom for life.[106] It is worth mentioning that Newbigin's theology was not always Trinitarian, but in fact was quite christocentric. However, as Newbigin's concern developed for reality outside of the church, there was a shift from a christocentric approach to mission to a Trinitarian understanding of mission.[107] For a practical theology that embraces all aspects of life, this Trinitarian perspective can aid us in the same way it did Newbigin. We will now examine how he understands the missional dimension of each person of the Trinity.

Proclaiming the Kingdom of the Father

Newbigin places the proclamation of God's reign over the whole of the cosmic universe as the starting point for mission:

> God is the creator, and consummator of all that is. We are not talking about one sector of human affairs, one strand out of the whole fabric of world history; we are talking about the reign and sovereignty of God over all that is, and therefore we are talking about the origin, meaning, and the end of the universe. We are not dealing with the local and temporary disturbance in the current cosmic happenings, but with the source and goal of the cosmos.[108]

The particularity of the election of Israel in the biblical story must be seen in the light of a blessing for the nations. This is not an other-worldly promise

---

105. Louw, *A Pastoral Hermeneutic*, 82, 84–85.
106. Newbigin, *The Open Secret*, 28.
107. Goheen, "As the Father," 65.
108. Newbigin, *The Open Secret*, 30.

or a means of escape; it has to do with the here and now.¹⁰⁹ Newbigin has been criticized for making this the starting point for his reflection on the Father, instead of the creation.¹¹⁰

The calling for God's dream to become manifest in the world is not a way of triumphal utopia, through the conquering and captivity of the world, but the way of the cross, suffering, pain, and humility. In the same way that the benefits of election for Israel were not for themselves, neither is the benefit of the resurrection for those who receive it, but for others. This story of God's reign and the Father's proclamation will not be a straightforward ride to victory, but one of "tribulation and faithful witness, of death and resurrection."¹¹¹ The logical outworking for mission is what Newbigin states as faith in action where,

> It is the acting out by proclamation and by endurance, through all the events of history, of the faith that the kingdom of God has drawn near. It is the acting out of the central prayer that Jesus taught his disciples to use: "Father, hallowed be thy name, thy kingdom come; thy will be done on earth as it is in heaven."¹¹²

Sharing the Life of the Son

In Jesus, the kingdom becomes present and manifest. The kingdom was not a distant hope, but now has a human face. A shift from proclaiming the kingdom became, for those after Jesus, one of proclaiming Jesus who was the embodiment of the kingdom. Of course, part of God's reign involves the forgiveness of sins and the reality of judgement. The reality of the kingdom calls for decisive action now.¹¹³ We ought also to embody the life of the kingdom in ourselves with the same commitment to action for God's kingdom. Newbigin further believes that, as Christians, we cannot lose the concept of God's wrath towards sin—correctly understood and appropriated.¹¹⁴

Despite this, questions regarding the cross, the wrath of God, and the atonement, seem to find scant reference in Newbigin's works. Goheen notes

109. Ibid., 32, 34.
110. Goheen, "As the Father," 133.
111. Newbigin, *The Open Secret*, 38.
112. Ibid., 39.
113. Ibid., 40–42, 44.
114. Ibid., 50.

that this might be due to his ecumenical tendencies that often led him "to frame controversial theological issues in terms that would challenge familiar divergences between traditions."[115]

For Newbigin it is important to realize that we cannot escape the fact that Jesus called to himself a community to be witness to the arrival of his reign—the church.[116] As already seen, I am wary to equate the kingdom with the church. Despite my hesitation, one must still attest to the reality that, in some way, the kingdom should be uniquely manifest in the church as it serves the world. Yet, this must always remain in tension with affirming that the kingdom is broader and, in some senses, exists without the church.

In speaking about the church's relationship to the kingdom, Newbigin notes:

> The church represents the presence of the reign of God in the life of the world, not in the triumphalist sense (as the successful cause) and not in the moralistic sense (as the righteous cause), but in the sense that it is the place where the mystery of the kingdom present in the dying and rising of Jesus is made present here and now so that all people, righteous and unrighteous, are enabled to taste and share the love of God before whom all are unrighteous and all are accepted as righteous.[117]

Bearing the Witness of the Spirit

Newbigin speaks of the Father as the proclamation of the kingdom and the Son as the presence of the kingdom.[118] He now refers to the Spirit as the prevenience of the kingdom. For Newbigin the Spirit's role is prior to, and necessary for, the church's work: "Mission is not just something that the church does; it is something that is done by the Spirit, who is himself the witness, who changes both the world and the church, who always goes before the church in its missionary journey."[119] Newbigin calls it "the very life-giving presence of God himself."[120] It is God's Spirit that launches the mission of the church at Pentecost and it still remains the Spirit's mission.

---

115. Goheen, "As the Father," 152.
116. Newbigin, *The Open Secret*, 52.
117. Ibid., 54.
118. Ibid., 56.
119. Ibid.
120. Ibid., 58.

It is the Spirit that shapes, changes, molds, and moves the nature and shape that mission takes.[121]

The church's witness is secondary to the witness of the Spirit, and to where the Spirit leads us.[122] The Spirit further brings a powerful witness to the reality of God's reign in the world.[123] The future of God's great dream for the world is caught up in the clash between the Spirit's work in the past and the movement of the future into the present:

> The Spirit brings the reality of the new world to come into the midst of the old world that is. It is the proof that we are heirs of the coming kingdom. And it is thus that the Spirit is witness—the recognizable presence of a future that has been promised but is not yet in sight. It is thus, also, that the Spirit is the source of hope—not just hope for ourselves, but hope for the completion of God's whole cosmic work.[124]

Reflecting on a Missional Triune God

After attempting to place the relevance of the Trinity for practical theological discourse, as well as briefly discussing the issue of the knowledge of God's being, we looked at the question of the *missio Dei* as understood by Newbigin. We noted the Father's proclaiming role, the Son's presence, and the Spirit's prevenience.

I believes that practical theology finds its basis and task in serving the Triune God's mission in the world. It indeed draws its theological reflection from God's activity in the world while, at the same time, is committed to participation in its ongoing missional activity. Practical theology, due to the wideness of God's mission, regards all of life as within the bounds of theological reflection. I believe a postfoundationalist approach, which will be fleshed out in more detail to come, can best serve this missional perspective within practical theology. Taking into account the reality of God's missional nature and its implications for practical theology, we shall now examine the concept of the church as missional.

---

121. Ibid., 59.
122. Ibid., 61.
123. Ibid., 63.
124. Ibid., 61.

Postfoundationalist Reflections in Practical Theology

The Missional Church and Practical Theology

If practical theology and theological reflection are committed to seeing God's reign reflected upon, and demonstrated in, the real world—the stuff of life—it must ask itself the missional question. Here, an attempt has been made to show how the missional question should be framed and placed in its historical context. It also attempted to show its roots in God's missional nature and activity. Practical theology ought to be committed to missional reflection and activity, because the Triune God is committed to missional activity. As we shall see in the next section, practical theology must give attention to the local. By doing this, it is consistent with a missional perspective while, at the same time, moving beyond foundationalism with its emphasis on the contextual nature of knowledge. Theological reflection ought to emerge from within faith communities and those who are involved in the local, real situations of life. This is in contrast to academies and denominational structures that provide the communities' theological reflection, already packaged and ready for application—the applied theology of foundationalism. Yet, it is my conviction that faith communities, with an incorrect understanding of the all-encompassing nature of mission, remain at present largely handicapped in their ability to respond to the challenges at hand. Therefore, a broader focus on mission would enable Christians within faith communities to see all of life as ready for analysis and reflection. It is based on the belief that all of life is redeemable and within the orbit of Christ's Lordship, and is open to the reality of the gospel's message and change. Simply stated, God is missional, therefore the church is missional. A quote from John Franke perhaps best illustrates this:

> The church is entrusted with the missional task of proclaiming and living out the gospel and its implications in the world. The nature of the church and its missional calling are tied up with the church's relationship with God and its role in the *missio Dei*. As suggested, God is social and missional in character, and these aspects of the divine nature have implications for the church and the task of theology.[125]

If the church is missional, it therefore gives itself in mission—and this has implications for its theology, as Franke notes. This means that the shape and task of the church should be related to its unique missional calling. We do not ask what a church should look like, but rather: What is the mission

---

125. Franke, *The Character of Theology*, 120.

A Postfoundationalist Practical Theology

for this specific church? Once the mission has been clarified, the *type*, *model*, or *structural* questions can be discussed. This would imply that our churches (and indeed theological reflection) would be vastly different according to the unique nature of the mission in which one is engaged.[126] The gospel (the good news that Jesus is Lord of the whole world), as it breaks into each unique situation as a result of God's missional activity to which the church has responded, would lead to different expressions of church life: unique mission, unique location, unique church, unique theological reflection. Vincent Donovan, who worked amongst the Masai, reminds us that, "While the general outline of the church is certainly present in Scripture, the specific details of the church, the response to the good news, will just as certainly have to be as free and diverse as all the separate cultures of the human race."[127]

Not only is the church (and practical theology) missional by nature, but also finds itself in a unique missional environment. The close relationship that the church enjoyed with the state, and all its benefits, has collapsed. This Christendom model resulted in what Shenk describes as a "church without mission."[128] Traditional Christian societies no longer view themselves as Christians. This reality has its roots in the Enlightenment, but has only really borne its fruit during the last century. Some have begun to speak about the desecularization of the West. But Ganzevoort[129] has argued, that even though this might be the case, the church still finds itself in a deinstitutionalized situation and on the fringes of society. The truth of the matter is that the Western world is now itself a mission field.[130] Christianity's precarious position within much of the world is further heightened by the huge shifts that have taken place in epistemology, which we have noted. The rejection of the modern Enlightenment project has created a uniquely challenging missional reality for the church. Hiebert comments that, in a "postmodern world we need to re-examine our epistemological foundations to see how they affect our relationships to other people, cultures, theologies, and religions in a pluralistic world. . . . I am also convinced it is the approach we must take in a postcolonial era in missions."[131]

---

126. Frost and Hirsch, *The Shaping of Things to Come*, 30.
127. Donovan, *Christianity Rediscovered*, 81–82.
128. Shenk, *Write the Vision*, 35.
129. Ganzevoort, "Teaching Religion," 119–20.
130. Newbigin, *The Open Secret*, 7.
131. Hiebert, *Anthropological Reflections*, 51.

This missional reality is one that practical theology will have to take into account. The specific consequences of this epistemological shift beyond foundationalism will be further fleshed out when we explore in what manner practical theology ought to approach its sources for theological reflection.

The Missional Church and Practical Theology?

James Fowler is perhaps best known for his work *Stages of Faith*. It is however perhaps his chapter written in *Practical Theology* entitled "Practical Theology: the Shaping of Christian Lives" that has had a significant influence on the development of modern day practical theology. Fowler states that: "Practical theology is theological reflection and construction arising out of and giving guidance to a community of faith in the praxis of its mission. Practical theology is critical and constructive reflection on the praxis of the Christian community's life and work in its various dimensions."[132] Therefore practical theology, and its reflection, does not take place in a vacuum. It arises out of, and gives guidance to, the community of faith and the individual Christians who comprise that community. If this community is stated to be missional by nature, derived from God's missional nature, its reflection should also be missional. Therefore, it discovers its mandate in the unique missional reality in which it finds itself. Practical theology is at the service of God's mission and his mission is local, and therefore, compatible with an approach to practical theology that is postfoundationalist. In the next section, we shall begin to examine what this local aspect of practical theology should look like, as we take the important issues of context and the local and combine them with global realities, and discuss the glocal nature of practical theology.

A GLOCAL PRAXIS-BASED PRACTICAL THEOLOGY

We have been discussing the missional nature of practical theology and have come to several conclusions that need to be restated. Firstly, mission by nature is holistic. It involves all the dimensions of life—individual, corporate, and cosmic. All of life is subject to God's missional activity. God's kingdom represents an understanding of mission that broadens *salvation*

---

132. Fowler, "Practical Theology," 149.

A Postfoundationalist Practical Theology

to include activity outside of the church, yet also near to it. The kingdom and church are held in creative tension. Practical theology, in service of God's mission, must take into account the individual, the corporate, and the cosmic. All of life is subject to theological reflection and action.

Secondly, God is missional by nature. He is on a mission and is the author and sustainer of mission. Therefore, practical theology is also, by nature, missional as it places itself in service of God's mission and dream for the earth. Practical theology is not the author and sustainer of mission, but rather a reflection upon, and an acting-with, God's mission.

Thirdly, God is missional, therefore the church is missional. The church responds to God's mission, and is sustained by him in mission. Because God is on a mission, the church is on a mission. The fact that the church is local implies that God's mission is unique according to each location, which then has implications for the shape and nature of the church. Practical theology, in the service of God and the church, therefore aids the church in its reflection and participation in God's mission. As the church's mission is local and particular, so practical theology is local and particular. Therefore, practical theology must begin its reflection with local realities and seek to ensure that its theoretical proposals have practical ramifications and outlets into these local realities. This is a missional practical theology that has indeed moved beyond foundationalism, which affirms the contextual nature of knowledge. This approach must be deepened.

The question must now be asked as to how one does this reflection. How do we reflect missionally and in a way that is consistent with a postfoundationalist approach? We reflect missionally by taking context into account. The local realities and stuff of life in which people are involved become the locus of God's mission. If God's mission is local, then theological reflection must begin with a pastoral concern.[133] Cronshaw explains De Kock's focus on the pastoral concern as follows:

> De Kock's method in vocational learning is to start with the students' questions that emerge from contemporary life and ministry practice rather than traditional answers and biblical sources. He is committed to sourcing appropriate theological responses from Scripture and Tradition, but wants to train students to start with the emerging questions of our time.[134]

---

133. De Kock, "Open Seminary at Tabor," 8.
134. Cronshaw, "Reenvisioning," 6.

Postfoundationalist Reflections in Practical Theology

If God's mission is local, and practical theology starts with a pastoral concern, then people's experience becomes a source for theology. The applied theology of foundationalism, whether based on an inerrant Bible or religious experience, will not work. Knowledge is contextual and emerges within a given reality. It is one of many factors brought into the theological conversation and is, in itself, the starting point.

If God's mission is local, and practical theology begins with a pastoral concern, then it requires an empirical analysis that is glocal (taking local and global factors into account). This missional activity of God in the local pastoral concern, taking people's experience into account, analyzed glocally and empirically, gives rise to pastoral reflection at a theoretical level, at which God's missional activity, or potential missional activity, is reflected upon where certain sources come into play. A correlational hermeneutic, whose epistemology is postfoundationalist, now takes both the Christian classics (biblical and historical) and the human and social sciences as sources for reflection. These sources are brought to bear on the experience of individuals, communities and the environment, which has arisen through glocal analysis. A theoretical proposal for a postfoundationalist glocal missional activity is now followed through with a proposal for, and indeed participation in, pastoral action. This participation in missional action has glocal implications. This process of pastoral concern, pastoral reflection, and pastoral action is then repeated as action gives rise to new experiences, upon which reflection is needed. This is consistent with the local contextual nature of knowledge for which a postfoundationalist approach calls. What has been described is known as the *pastoral cycle*. I believe that the pastoral cycle could best represent a move beyond foundationalism. This will now be explored in more detail.

The Pastoral Cycle

There are various ways of framing what is meant by the pastoral cycle. In the short introduction to this section, I have already hinted at how I understand it. In Ballard and Pritchards' book *Practical Theology in Action*, they divided practical theology into four models with various sub-divisions. The broad categories were: applied theology, correlational hermeneutics, praxis, and *habitus*. The pastoral cycle was regarded as being central to the praxis model, yet having equal importance within the correlational model.[135] In

---

135. Ballard and Pritchard, *Practical Theology*, 71.

terms of some form of methodological consensus, they regarded the pastoral cycle as a unifying factor. Ballard and Pritchard comment as follows: "The pastoral cycle has become widely used in practical theology, and there are a number of variations on the theme. . . . Such widespread acceptance clearly suggests that the pastoral cycle should be at the heart of any contemporary perspective on practical theology."[136]

The pastoral cycle has many roots but, in contemporary practical theology, it certainly has found its impetus from the influence of liberation theology.[137] Throughout the discussion on praxis that follows, one will notice a return again and again to the work of the liberation theologian, Clodovis Boff, and his work, *Theology and Praxis*. Although torturous at times, and certainly not easy reading, he attempts to look intensively at the complex relationship between theory and praxis and, in many ways, demonstrates the use of this pastoral cycle.

Graham et al. place the pastoral cycle's roots, developed by liberation theology, in the Young Christian Workers' see-judge-act method. It was also in the work of Juan-Luis Segundo's *The Liberation of Theology*, informed by Paul Ricoeur's hermeneutics, that the pastoral cycle was popularized.[138] It is no coincidence that, like Ballard and Pritchard, Graham et al. have placed the pastoral cycle under the praxis model, or what they call "theology in action."

We noted that Ballard and Pritchard feel that the pastoral cycle has a unifying dimension for various practical theological models—especially the correlational and the praxis models. It is no wonder then that Don Browning, who developed a critical correlational model, in fact adheres in many ways to this pastoral cycle.[139] A quote from him perhaps best affords us a definition of what we mean by the pastoral cycle: "The view I propose goes from practice to theory and back to practice. Or more accurately, it goes from present theory-laden practice to a retrieval of normative theory-laden practice to the creation of more critically held theory-laden practices."

This pastoral cycle is not dissimilar to the theological reflection that James and Evelyn Whitehead propose in their book, *Method in Ministry: Theological Reflection and Christian Ministry*, published in 1995. They propose a three-step process similar to the see-judge-act, or the

---

136. Ibid., 82–83.
137. Ibid., 82.
138. Graham et al., *Theological Reflection*, 188.
139. Browning, *A Fundamental Practical Theology*, 7.

practice-theory-action process for which the pastoral cycle argues. The process they propose is one of attending, asserting, and then pastoral response.[140] One attends to a specific experience or practice that is then brought into dialogue with the Christian tradition and culture where an assertion is made, which in turn leads to a pastoral response. Here, the term "pastoral concern," taken from the Whiteheads, has been used when discussing the first part of the pastoral cycle. The term "pastoral action," similar to the Whitehead's term "pastoral response," but borrowed from De Kock, has also been used. De Kock has developed a form of theological reflection in what is known as "open seminary." Here, he essentially works with, adapts, and actually fleshes out, the Whiteheads' methodology. He chooses to call the term "pastoral response" "pastoral action." This is done intentionally to show that the pastoral cycle must not end in a theoretical proposal for action, but must go beyond that and move to an intervention, or action.[141] Poling's description of practical theology demonstrates this pastoral cycle whereby he advocates a "rhythm between practice-based reflection and systematic theological reflection. Practices stimulate theological reflection, and theological reflection shapes the development of practices."[142]

So, what does it mean to begin one's theological reflection with a pastoral concern? It means that certain local and global factors ought to be taken into account. It also affirms the importance of experience as a source for theological reflection, as well as the value of social analysis or research. These will all now be discussed separately.

The Local Dimension of Practical Theology

Essential to understanding the local nature of theology is to admit from the outset that an applied practical theology, a theology from above that is trans-historical and simply downloaded onto a local situation, is indeed a thing of a foundationalist past. For, as Hendriks notes, "If Christianity really wants to engage the hearts and minds of believers, it must seriously regard the context that shapes their lives and in which their communities are rooted."[143] By arguing for the starting point of theology in the local, we

---

140. Whitehead and Whitehead, *Method in Ministry*, 13.
141. De Kock, "Open Seminary at Tabor," 9.
142. Poling, "Constructive Practical Theology," 199.
143. Hendriks, *Studying Congregations in Africa*, 27.

A Postfoundationalist Practical Theology

reject "theological debate which proceeds as if abstracted from the total situation in which reflection takes place."[144] By arguing for the local nature of theology, we agree with Segundo that there is no "autonomous, impartial, academic theology floating free above the realm of human options and biases."[145] Theology does not begin in the academy, but in reality—in the experiences of "individuals and communities."[146] It resists a form of abstract theology.[147]

This means that theological reflection must begin with the *stuff* of people's lives. The word "praxis" is controversial. Bevans sees praxis as *action in reflection* and defines it in the following manner:

> It is reflected-upon action and acted-upon reflection—both rolled into one. Practitioners of the praxis model believe that in this concept of praxis they have found a new and profound way that, more than all others, is able to deal adequately with the experience of the past (Scripture and tradition) and the experience of the present (human experience, culture, social location, and social change).[148]

Bevans rejects an understanding of praxis that equates it simply with practice. He notes its roots in Marxism, the Frankfurt school, and Paulo Freire. For Bevans, it is rather a method and model of thinking. It seems that others would agree (e.g., Hendriks[149] and W. de Kock). De Kock views praxis as the interaction and tension between theory and practice where true knowledge lies. Kim has noted the roots of praxis in Aristotle's thinking, "where theory and practice are intertwined, and where *praxis* referred to a purposeful and reflective action initiated through engagement in social situations."[150] Clodovis Boff also argues for a tension between theory and practice.[151] In fact, he argues that even though they are to be differentiated, it is artificial when one tries to separate the two. Yet, it seems that despite Boff speaking of praxis as "human activity to transform the world"[152]

---

144. Bonino, *Revolutionary Theology*, 86.
145. Segundo, *Liberation of Theology*, 13.
146. Cochrane et al., *In Word and in Deed*, 17.
147. Kretzschmar, "Ethics in a Theological Context," 4.
148. Bevans, *Models of Contextual Theology*, 71–72.
149. Hendriks, *Studying Congregations in Africa*, 22; De Kock, "Open Seminary at Tabor," 9.
150. Kim, "The Hermeneutical-Praxis Paradigm," 421.
151. Boff, *Theology and Praxis*, 213.
152. Ibid., 210.

(which includes a theoretical dimension), he still uses praxis in a *practical sense* as the starting point for theological reflection. In the following quote, Boff argues for praxis as holding primacy as a starting point for theology:

> It must first of all be acknowledged that praxis holds the primacy over theory. This primacy is of an analytical, not an ethical, character. It is not to be understood as one of mechanical causality, but precisely of dialectical causality. It defines how the one factor is the prime, material condition for the existence of the other. Praxis is *de facto* the comprehensive element of theory; as such it constitutes the space where theory is localized and defined, the space where it arises, develops, and comes to completion.[153]

Although affirming the importance of the local for theological reflection, Boff cautions against equating the local situation as truth. Practical effectiveness, or a pragmatism that rejects theoretical reflection, is rejected. For Boff, the local practice of something does not assign a "moral qualification"[154] to it. He argues that taking local practice into account at the expense of theory is to the detriment of praxis itself.[155]

Here, we are perhaps getting ahead of ourselves. The point that is attempted is that the starting point of the pastoral cycle must begin with the practice of real life. It cannot start by taking abstract ideas and seek to work them out in local realities. As noted repeatedly throughout this work, a postfoundationalist approach to practical theology must emphasize these local realities, as knowledge is contextual and fluid. Müller describes it thus:

> The postfoundationalist approach forces us to firstly listen to the stories of people in real life situations. It hasn't got the aim of merely describing a general context, but of confronting us with a specific and concrete situation. This approach, although also hermeneutical in nature, moves beyond mere hermeneutics. It is more reflexive and situationally embedded in epistemology and methodology.[156]

Practical theology must begin its dialectical process by listening to the *emerging questions*[157] that arise out of the daily cultural realities of human

---

153. Ibid., 215.
154. Ibid., 202.
155. Ibid., 198.
156. Müller, "Transversal Rationality," 5.
157. Cronshaw, "Reenvisioning Theological Education," 6; De Kock, "Open Seminary at Tabor," 8.

A Postfoundationalist Practical Theology

beings and the church. It takes seriously the current issues of the day.[158] Praxis "prepares the agenda, the repertory of questions, that theology is to address."[159]

We have realized that by arguing for the local nature of theology, we argue for a contextual theology. Bevans points out the importance of contextual theology today.[160] He notes the dissatisfaction and suspicion of the third world toward first world theology, which has overpowered them and forced them to deal with realities irrelevant to their daily lives. Along with the growing identity of local churches, the oppressive nature of the older approaches that neglected and, in fact, attacked legitimate cultural expressions, has also been rejected.[161]

Bevans also reminds us of the theological underpinnings of a local theology in the idea of the incarnation, as well as the affirmation of the sacramental nature of theology (where all of life is seen as a locus of God's presence and activity).[162] The importance of the broad dimension of mission in practical theology, as mentioned already, has obvious parallels in discussing theology's sacramental nature. The nature of divine revelation as present in believers' daily lives,[163] the catholicity of the church in championing the local, and the Triune God's active, present, and dynamic role in day-to-day realities, are all affirmed as important.[164]

The importance of contextualization for theology is worked out in the pastoral cycle. Segundo describes this as the hermeneutical circle that begins with experienced reality—a real context.[165] When discussing contextualization, Bosch also refers to this dialectical relationship between theory and practice that has its roots in praxis, or experience.[166]

However, Bosch cautions contextual theologians about viewing God as totally wrapped up in the historical process.[167] Further dangers involve uncritical celebration of a variety of often exclusive theologies, which can

---

158. Chopp, "Educational Process," 115.
159. Boff, *Theology and Praxis*, 200.
160. Bevans, *Models of Contextual Theology*, 9.
161. Ibid., 10.
162. Ibid., 12.
163. Ibid., 14.
164. Ibid., 15.
165. Segundo, *Liberation of Theology*, 9.
166. Bosch, *Transforming Mission*, 425.
167. Ibid., 427–28.

often lead to absolutism. When taking these concerns into account, one must not allow the contextual and local realties to determine the truth of theology. What we are affirming here though, is that a theology that is divorced from local realities remains irrelevant and subject to potential ideological captivity and foundationalist assumptions. To realize God's presence in history and to begin with local issues means that we can begin the process of dialogue from the correct starting point. However, for a theologian to be local, he or she must identify, participate, and give voice to the experience of the local situation out of which his or her theology arises.

Experience as Source

Many are aware of John Wesley's quadrilateral, in which he posits four sources that need to be taken into account when conducting theological reflection. They are: experience, tradition, reason and Scripture. Grenz cautions against the use of experience as a source for theology and sees it rather as the medium through which sources are received.[168] However, he does argue that just because it is not normative for theology, does not make it irrelevant.[169] In his elevation of culture as a source of theology, he might in fact be engaging with people's experience as a source, without knowing it. Again, we do not argue that one's experience is true, but again affirm that experience must be our starting point. James Cone is one who argues that black experience should be one's starting point when doing local and contextual theology.[170] Chung Hyun Kyung, who attempts to delineate what an Asian women's theology should look like, elevates Asian women's experience as a starting point when beginning theological reflection. A quote from her best illustrates what we mean by experience as the starting point for theological reflection:

> Asian women's theology was born out of Asian women's tears and sighs and from their burning desire for liberation and wholeness. It is neither the logical consequence of academic debate of the university nor the pastoral conclusion of the institutional church. Asian women's theology has emerged from Asian women's cries and screams, from the extreme suffering of their everyday lives. They have shouted from pain when their own and their children's

---

168. Grenz, *Theology for the Community of God*, 15.
169. Ibid., 17.
170. Cone, *Teologia Nera*, 23.

bodies collapsed from starvation, rape, and battering. Theological reflection has emerged as a response to women's suffering.[171]

Someone's experience, or one's own personal experience, gives birth to the pastoral concern that begins the pastoral cycle for practical theology. Of necessity, this raises the question as to the location of the theologian or *theological reflector*. Can practical theology be done without some form of engagement by the one doing the theological reflecting? Clodovis Boff gives three ways in which a theologian can be engaged with the theological process. Before doing this, however, he makes some presuppositional comments around the idea of *engagement* that must be taken into account when discussing experience as a starting point for theological reflection.

The truth is that one need not begin theological reflection from experience or the local to be *engaged*.[172] Indeed, by nature, everyone is engaged to some extent and all theologians "do theology in and from some determinate social locus."[173] An engaged theology can be *traditionalist* or *progressive* and its content is usually defined according to one's ideological position.[174] There are also important distinctions and overlaps between practical engagement and theoretical engagement.[175] The three types of engagement that Boff lists with regard to local and experiential realities are as follows.

The Specific Contribution Model

Here, engagement is done at a theoretical level where intellectual positions are taken on behalf of a group or individual's local experience.[176] However, pure theory can only have practical implications through practical participation. By this, Boff means that one ought to have certain channels and opportunities to engage with the experience and local reality that one seeks to represent.[177]

---

171. Chung, *Struggle to Be the Sun Again*, 22.
172. Boff, *Theology and Praxis*, 160.
173. Ibid., 159.
174. Ibid., 161.
175. Ibid., 168.
176. Ibid.
177. Ibid., 169.

Postfoundationalist Reflections in Practical Theology

The Alternating Moments Model

This might be seen as a sort of dualism—the theoretical and practical moments coincide. In one moment, the theologian is reflecting; yet, in the other moment, he is participating in the actual lived experience of a group of which the reflection forms part. It is not so much a dualism as it is, rather, a series of alternating movements of the one who is engaging.[178]

The Incarnational Model

Here, one does not so much identify with a specific group, and participate in that lived experience, as much as one actually is joined in the "general life condition and lot of the group in question."[179] In certain circumstances, this sort of identification might make theological reflection difficult in terms of materials at one's disposal.[180]

These three models provide a picture of what sort of engagement is necessary for theological reflection that is local and takes into account experience as a starting point for theology. It is important that we realize that practical theology does not take place in a vacuum, and is somehow privy to some sort of theological and experiential neutrality. In what has been discussed, it might appear that a position has been taken that states that, unless someone is part of, or sympathetic to, a specific local context and experiential dynamic, they cannot do good theology. It might appear that, unless someone is bound within a specific pastoral concern, they are really unable to be truly concerned. Bevans says the following in this regard:

> A person can in several significant but limited ways contribute to the contextualisation of theology in a context that is not his or her own. But when a person does this, he or she must approach the host culture with both humility and honesty. He or she must have humility because he or she will always be on the margins of the society in which he or she has chosen to work.[181]

What Bevans says of cultures applies equally to any specific pastoral concern that practical theology uses as a starting point. For this reason, Hendriks places such emphasis on the fact that the laity and believers ought to

178. Ibid., 170.
179. Ibid.
180. Ibid., 171.
181. Bevans, *Models of Contextual Theology*, 21.

be "producers of theology."[182] For this reason, the best form of theological reflection on the church and her practical engagement flows from those who are actually engaged in that church, the contextual dynamics, and lived experience of that community.

Here, the argument has been for the local nature of practical theology as it best illustrates a postfoundationalist approach to theological reflection. It is a practical theology that places high value on experience as a starting point and source for theological reflection. It is a practical theology that seeks to take the local seriously by identifying or participating with the lived experience of a particular group or individual. At this point, it would be unwise not to bring the global nature of practical theology into the discussions. The local situation with the lived experience of that local group has, at the same time, a global influence to it. A simple analysis and understanding of the local might provide a skewed picture of what is happening, and even the possibility to bring about change might be thwarted. Financial markets and policies on different continents can have a vast and long-lasting impact on the local situation in which one finds oneself. Ideological currents and economic instability can radically alter one's lived experience. In taking into account the local nature of theology, we must also take into account the global. This tension of analysis the researcher has chosen to call the *glocal* (local and global) nature of practical theology and theological reflection. With specific reference to Africa, Hendriks speaks of the global dimension of practical theology:

> In doing theology in Africa, we must be realistic about our situation in Africa. Theology should study the global, social, economic, political megatrends and how they influence our continent. What are the national and local realities with which we should deal?[183]

The Glocal Nature of Practical Theology

We have been focusing on practical theology's local nature, as well as the importance of experience as a starting point for theological reflection. Any analysis of one's local situation and its contextual realities must take into account global dynamics that are brought to bear upon one's situation. Bonino shows how Latin America has been at the mercy of outside factors

---

182. Hendriks, *Studying Congregations in Africa*, 26.
183. Ibid., 27.

from the very beginning of colonial times.[184] The lust for wealth and power in Spain saw the local people's culture destroyed and desecrated. Even later when independence was gained from Spain, the ruling classes connived with foreign banks, countries, and institutions to bring about new levels of exploitation and an era of neo-colonialism.[185] Global factors, of which one has no control, affected people's local context and helped to define their experience and identity. Bonino shows how the capitalist form of production has had adverse effects on the dependent countries.[186] Bonino was writing in the 1970s and could not have foreseen to what extent technology would add to the unfettered march of capitalism. This, certainly, is not an argument for any sort of Communism or Socialism, but merely points out what sociologists such as Manuel Castells, have been showing us.

Castells points out that the world in which we live has become globalized to the extent that our whole social landscape has changed. "Our world, and our lives, are being shaped by the conflicting trends of globalization and identity. The information technology revolution, and the restructuring of capitalism, have induced a new form of society, the network society."[187] Individuals, groups, and regions that do not service the goals of this network society are simply ignored or "switched off".[188] The intense and changing global world in which we live has resulted in massive insecurity for many.

> In a world of global flows of wealth, power, and images, the search for identity, collective and individual, ascribed or constructed, becomes the fundamental source of social meaning. . . . Identity is becoming the main, and sometimes the only, source of meaning since in an historical period characterized by widespread destructuring of organisations, delegitimation of institutions, fading away of major social movements, and ephemeral cultural expressions.[189]

Globalization is a fact. The reaction against globalization, in the rise of national (not state) identities, is testament to this. Therefore, it is only logical that a practical theology that has experience as a starting point, and one seeking to be local, must at the same time give due attention to global factors. It must be a glocal practical theology. It must ask questions as to what

184. Bonino, *Revolutionary Theology*, 5.
185. Ibid., 16.
186. Ibid., 31.
187. Castells, *The Information Age*, 1.
188. Ibid., 3.
189. Ibid.

A Postfoundationalist Practical Theology

economic, cultural, political, and social realities in the rest of the world are impacting on one's local reality. Segundo says this is part of the suspicion toward ideological superstructures arising out of one's experience that ought to be challenged. This could be worked out in a myriad of ways. The local clothing industry in the Cape could collapse due to the rising power of China. Inflation, with its impact on local households and their ability to feed themselves, has its roots in conflicts in the Middle East, monopolies and speculators.

Practical theology certainly has seen a move to the local in the last quarter of the twentieth century, as already discussed. However, this return to the local must take into account global factors that impinge on people's identities and experience, noting the "increasingly interconnected character of all human, political, economic, and social life on earth."[190]

But, how do we go about understanding this glocal context? How do we take into account experience as a starting point, while trying to get to grips with local and global factors that influence that experience? What is called for is some form of social analysis.

Social Analysis

Don Browning's fundamental practical theology argues for four movements within practical theology. Here, the first movement concerns us, which is what he calls "descriptive theology." Descriptive theology is linked directly to what has just been discussed regarding the glocal nature of practical theology with its starting point in experience. Browning describes it as follows:

> Its task is more important than its name. It is to describe the contemporary theory-laden practices that give rise to the practical questions that generate all theological reflection. To some extent, this first movement is horizon analysis; it attempts to analyse the horizon of cultural and religious meanings that surround our religious and secular practices.[191]

This desire to begin with descriptive theology, by necessity, implies the importance of social analysis. The human sciences are directly linked to descriptive theology in their role of determining the concrete reality that will, at a later point, be brought into dialogue with the Christian sources.[192]

190. Hendriks, *Studying Congregations in Africa*, 27.
191. Browning, *A Fundamental Practical Theology*, 47.
192. Ibid., 92–93.

Gerben Heitink[193] takes into account the anthropological shift in theology, characterized by the empirical shift in practical theology since the 1960s.[194] We have demonstrated this shift and its importance for practical theology in the first part of this work. None would doubt that there has been this empirical shift in practical theology, but we do need some perspective on this issue, which I think Heimbrock provides us with:

> the empirical interest within theology it is neither an invention nor the sole property of practical theology. "Empirical theology" as an explicit and programmatic formula has been labeled in the beginning of the 20th century, in remarkable theological efforts on both sides of the Atlantic. And this happened long before practical theology got its present form.[195]

Heitink, like Browning, believes the empirical data, which the social sciences uncover, is of utmost importance for theological reflection. This leads him to "an empirically orientated practical theology, which opts for a point of departure in the actual experiences of people and the situation of church and society, and is characterized by a theorizing approach that attempts to do full justice to empirical data."[196]

Boff sets out to demonstrate the importance of social analysis and the role of the human sciences for theological reflection. Although his work focuses mainly on the role they offer with regard to political theology, the insights are still of real use. Like those already mentioned, he affirms that a theology orientated toward practice must take into account the sciences of the social. This becomes important in what Boff calls "a socio-analytic mediation."[197] The importance of the use of the social sciences is not just to gain a correct understanding of a given situation, but to help theology to avoid the abstract speculation that endangers real change. Boff puts it graphically in the following manner: "The interfacing of theology with praxis through the medium of socio-analytic mediation has as its objective the safeguarding of theology from the empty 'theorism' that, in certain circumstances, is a trait of academic cynicism that ignores the crying scandal of the starving and suffering multitudes of our world."[198]

---

193. Heitink, *Practical Theology*, 22–21.
194. Ibid., 220.
195. Heimbrock, "Practical Theology," 155.
196. Heitink, *Practical Theology*, 221.
197. Boff, *Theology and Praxis*, 6.
198. Ibid., 7.

This must serve as a constant reminder that the use of the social sciences is not just for methodological integrity, but also has real people and their real situations as its focus. The social sciences, however, are not devoid of ideology with regard to both content and method. This will form an important part of our discussion later when the religious nature of the social sciences will be examined. At this point, we should note some of the obstacles that one encounters when discussing the importance of the social sciences. Boff mentions five, which we shall briefly discuss and acknowledge.

Empiricism

Here, the importance of social analysis is argued against on the basis that the issues are self-evident and the concerns are immediate. Lacking social analysis here can lead to multiple misunderstandings as to what is actually taking place.[199] Natural scientific knowledge must form the basis of theological cognition. Those who claim that the facts are self-evident, and that no non-theological disciplines are therefore needed, might simply get caught up in "certain current, ideological images that common sense forms of facts."[200]

Methodological Purism

Here, socio-analytical mediation is excluded on the basis that theology has its own proper status and has no need of other disciplines.[201] This does not take into account that theology, by its very nature, has arisen out of social reality and is socially mediated. Boff rejects this option and argues that theology ought to assume that it takes the raw material of life into account and seeks to do so critically.[202]

Theologism

In many ways, theologism is linked to methodological purism in the sense of claiming theology's unique and independent status. Here, theology

199. Ibid., 21.
200. Ibid., 22.
201. Ibid., 24.
202. Ibid., 25.

believes it possesses within its storehouse, all the resources necessary to comment on any given situation—whether political or otherwise.[203] It has its roots in a view of the world that argues for the transcendent nature of truth and a deeply sceptical attitude to real life.[204] Boff argues against theologism believing that one must take into account the silent prerequisites that the social sciences afford us in understanding reality.[205]

Semantic Mix

Here, the insights of the social sciences are not so much discarded as they are not integrated critically or properly.[206] On the one hand, the information is taken into the theological discourse without proper attention to its role. On the other hand, things that emerged from the analysis, which one cannot tolerate or accept, are replaced by more spiritual content. It seeks to collapse the tension into either corner instead of seeking to hold the insights of the social sciences in creative tension.[207]

Bilingualism

Bilingualism is related to that of semantic mix and it is quite difficult to distinguish between the two. Essentially, what happens here is that the social sciences and theology interact on the same *field*, yet speak two different *languages*. What happens in this scenario is that one of the different languages will seek to overcome the other and force it aside.[208]

A Way Forward?

Boff believes that a healthy relationship and appropriation of the social sciences are possible despite these difficulties and objections.[209] He believes that theology ought to understand that its formal object must be

203. Ibid., 26.
204. Ibid., 27.
205. Ibid., 26.
206. Ibid., 28.
207. Ibid.
208. Ibid., 29.
209. Ibid., 30.

distinguished by its material object. In other words, what emerges from the social sciences is not theology in the proper sense of the word. He explains it in the following manner:

> The sciences of the social furnish theology only with that upon which to ply its practice. Thus what for the sciences of the social is a product, finding, or construct, will be taken up in the theological field as raw material, as something to be (re)worked by procedures proper to theologizing, in such wise as to issue in a specifically theological product, and one so characterized.[210]

The importance of the social sciences for practical theology cannot be disputed, despite the objections, which we have just examined with Boff's help. Of course, there are dangers inherent in the use of the social sciences. Boff himself has called for theology as a theoretical discipline to be aware of, and shaped, according to its own grammar. The truth is that practical theology today has unanimously accepted the importance of the social sciences—and perhaps uncritically so. Browning argues that we might have done so without taking into account the ideological bent of the social sciences and, indeed, the researcher's situatedness. To this we now turn.

The Religious Dimension of the Social Sciences

The title of this short section could have been put under a different heading. It might have been called the *ideological* dimension of social sciences—for this could certainly be the case. However, the term Don Browning[211] uses in discussing the social sciences—that of its religious nature—was chosen to be used.

We have already affirmed the importance of the social sciences for practical theology, as well as certain obstacles in terms of how the relationship between theological reflection and the sciences can be related. Browning helps us to examine the hidden prejudices and ideological presuppositions that often lie hidden within the human sciences, which should urge caution on their unrestricted and uncritical appropriation. As already noted, Browning believes that theological reflection's first task is of a descriptive nature, which includes the use of psychology, sociology, economics, anthropology and a range of other disciplines.[212]

210. Ibid., 31.
211. Browning, *A Fundamental Practical Theology*, 89.
212. Ibid., 77.

Postfoundationalist Reflections in Practical Theology

Browning reminds us that the very research that takes place in an attempt to describe or understand what is happening is influenced by the historicity and ideological assumptions to which researchers are bound in their historical situatedness.[213] Browning describes this situatedness in terms of its religious dimension. It is religious in the sense of having pre-understandings and prejudices that have an effective history:

> If the social and human sciences are rooted in a tradition, if that tradition inevitably influences their interpretive perspectives (their pre-understanding and prejudices), and if that tradition has religious dimensions, does it follow that the interpretive horizon of the social sciences is colored by the religio-cultural backgrounds of the researchers?[214]

This religious and pre-suppositional awareness is something that was not addressed here, when emphasizing experience and the local as a starting point for theological reflection and central to a postfoundationalist approach. For, as one begins one's research, certain decisions as to what experience and what local situation one will examine is made at the expense of another local situation and experience. What pastoral concern does one concern oneself with? What does one remain unconcerned about? It would be foolish to think that one's ideological predispositions do not, in some way, govern one's choice. Segundo notes that this problem described here with regard to an individual researcher is, in fact, a much larger problem within the discipline of sociology itself. "Present-day sociology is retreating from the realms of human social life that are of increasing importance and simply refusing to deal with them. For our purposes here the important point is that they are the very realms which are most important."[215]

Browning believes that the best way to do this is to bring these religious assumptions and hidden implicit values into the light right at the beginning.[216] If the investigator does not do so, it will influence what is seen and indeed how that is evaluated. Browning's caution in the use of the social sciences should, in no way, be seen as devaluing their use within the theological context, but rather arguing that what is implicit in the human sciences becomes explicit in theological reflection. In that way, "the human sciences can be used within descriptive theology and their explanatory in-

---

213. Ibid., 81.
214. Ibid., 89.
215. Segundo, *Liberation of Theology*, 48.
216. Browning, *A Fundamental Practical Theology*, 91.

terests employed to account for biological, psychological, and sociological factors that influence but do not determine human behaviour. Here they would function within an explicit theological context, not unlike how they function within their implicit religious contexts in the human sciences as such." Taking into account Browning's cautions and Boff's obstacles to the use of the human sciences, we will now begin to look specifically at certain methodologies in terms of how we uncover the "raw material" for theological reflection.[217]

Research Methods

This is an entire field in and of itself. I cannot hope to give a definitive, or indeed even an overview, of this deep and complex subject. In this section I hope to relate the reality of a postfoundationalist perspective and its implications for research methods. We have been discussing the importance of the local dimension of practical theology and how experience is a critical source and starting point for practical theology. If foundationalism was driven by a quest for certainty and an applied theological approach what does that mean for researching the concrete and local realities in postfoundationalism? This has enormous implications for one's approach to social science methodology. If practical theology is not an applied theology based on foundationalism, but rather postfoundationalist, it simply has to engage with the social sciences in order to engage with specific local context to uncover and understand that is going in within that context. It is perhaps worth noting at this point Cameron et al.'s reflection that the practical theologian, having to be skilled as "practitioner, social scientist, theologian and cultural expert is in danger of becoming an impossible person!"[218] However due to its focus on specific situations, practical theology simply has to get to grips with the social sciences and research methodology. Swinton and Mowat believe that due to its focus on the local and specific, practical theology will need to enter into discussions with regard:

> to the various methods through which this knowledge is captured, analysed, understood and recorded. Historically, the primary mode of analysis and data collection has emerged from a continuing dialogue with the social sciences. The social sciences have offered practical theologians vital access to the nature of the human

217. Ibid., 92.
218. Cameron et al., *Talking about God in Practice*, 26.

mind, human culture, the wider dimensions of Church life and the implications of the social and political dimensions of society for the process of theological reflection.[219]

Cartledge, like Swinton and Mowat already mentioned, believes that theology cannot do without the human sciences—especially the empirical sciences: "practical theology, with its orientation of engagement with real people in real contexts, the need to use empirical approaches is fundamental to the discipline. Theoretical and abstract discussion also remain essential but they are used primarily in relation to empirical and concrete studies of people."[220] Taking into account that sociology cannot be value-free, and that such an idea is clearly at its end point in a postfoundationalist world, Cartledge has set out to chart a way forward with regard to methodology.[221] Cartledge borrows heavily from the work of Van der Ven, who argues for an intra-disciplinarial approach for practical theology, which adds some of the tools and instruments that the empirical sciences offer into its repertoire.[222] Heitink speaks of Van der Ven's intradisciplinary approach as an attempt to give maximum credit to social scientific research and encourage practical theologians to become conversant with social scientific methodology.[223]

Yet not only do we need to become conversant with social science methodology, but we need to understand the epistemological assumptions that underlie much social science research. These discussions require us to pay attention to what one chooses in terms of research. As mentioned earlier, this decision is thwarted by the ideological and interest-driven approach in terms of what is chosen for reflection. Heimbrock comments on this by noting that: "any serious empirical based theory does not simply apply to 'facts,' but inevitably bases its propositions upon large theoretical concepts, such as reality, life, and religion. Even the so-called starting points of data, empirical findings, or phenomena carry a heavy theoretical load."[224]

Although focusing on a more academic setting in terms of conducting research, Heitink provides a helpful starting point by arguing that research should ask the questions: Why, what, where and how? Further questions for the researchers to ask themselves are what they can handle, their limitations,

219. Swinton and Mowat, *Practical Theology*, vi.
220. Cartledge, *Practical Theology*, 11.
221. Ibid.
222. Ibid., 15.
223. Heitink, *Practical Theology*, 174.
224. Heimbrock, "From Data to Theory," 280.

and their competence. At this point, one must also begin to ask what type of research is best suited to the area one hopes to examine, and the question of qualitative or quantitative research.[225]

As mentioned earlier there is also a need to come to grips with ones epistemological issues when choosing ones area of research. This is critical for a postfoundationalist approach. Mason believes clarifying these issues early on in the research process is crucial, and that certain epistemologies are more consistent with different types of qualitative research itself, as well as with either qualitative or quantitative research.[226] This speaks directly to questions of knowledge and understanding and the issues of foundationalism. Questions of how we know things and the certainty of that knowledge. Mason speaks to this directly by noting that:

> Your epistemology is, literally, your theory of knowledge, and should therefore concern the principles and rules by which you decide whether and how social phenomena can be known, and how knowledge can be demonstrated. Different epistemologies have different things to say about these issues, and about what the status of knowledge can be. For some, the concept of evidence itself is to categorical, implying as it does that research can provide self-evidential proof of universally perceived objective realities, instead of the more epistemologically modest concepts of perspective and argument.[227]

This examining of one's own fundamental assumptions around the nature of truth and knowledge can be unsettling.[228] Baranov's work *Conceptual Foundations of Social Research Methods* is an attempt to show how different understandings regarding the nature of reality, and what can be known about that reality, has vast implications with regard to the type of methodology ones uses and the outcomes that can be gained from different research methods. For Baranov the challenge of antifoundationalism raises "fundamental questions about the ability of human reason to produce reliable knowledge about the social world."[229] This has significant implications for practical theology and theology in general, specifically with regard to qualitative research as Swinton and Mowat comment in that the:

225. Heitink, *Practical Theology*, 224, 226–28.
226. Mason, *Qualitative Researching*, 16.
227. Ibid.
228. Baronov, *Conceptual Foundations*, 5.
229. Ibid., 7.

"inherent tendency of qualitative research to assume a fundamentally nonfoundational epistemology which is highly sceptical about the possibility of accessing truth that has any degree of objectivity, stands in uneasy tension with the theological assumption that truth is available and accessible through revelation."[230]

Van Huyssteen[231] agrees that "nonfoundationalism will present a very real challenge to the Christian concept of revelation."[232] Baranov believes antifoundationalism poses several challenges for social research. These challenges are the rejection of models as accurate representations of reality, the neutrality of knowledge, the rejection of knowledge claims as universal findings and the danger of generalizing individual case studies. As we have seen, Van Huyysteen believes these challenges can be met by an approach which resists embracing antifoundationalism or foundationalism. Rather a "postfoundationalist shift to a fallibist epistemology, which honestly embraces the role of traditioned experience, personal commitment, interpretation, and the provisional nature of all our knowledge claims, avoids the alleged necessity of opting for either foundationalism or antifoundationalism."[233] I will later explore aspects of a correlational hermeneutic. At that juncture I will enter into discussions regarding certain epistemological underpinnings that underlie the human sciences in general. At this point I would simply like to point out that even the various methodologies one chooses to analyze experience in any given local context is theory laden as it "is impossible to carry out observations that are uncontaminated by theory."[234]

Any desire to understand one's local context will need to use the broad perspectives of either qualitative and quantitative research, or both. How do these differing ideas of research, and the diversity of methods within them, reflect the shift to a postfoundationalist perspective, and the implications of that, which van Huyssteen has just highlighted?[235]

Traditionally these questions of have revolved around the broad discussion of qualitative and quantitative research already mentioned. Dreyer believes that the fruitless debate between which method is better is a thing

230. Swinton and Mowat. *Practical Theology*, 73.
231. van Huyssteen, *Essays in Postfoundationalist Theology*, 226.
232. Baranov, *Conceptual Foundations*, 169–70.
233. van Huyssteen, *Essays in Postfoundationalist Theology*, 228.
234. Baranov, *Conceptual Foundations*, 69.
235. van Huyssteen, *Essays in Postfoundationalist Theology*, 228.

A Postfoundationalist Practical Theology

of the past and that most would agree that different methods are appropriate to differing contexts.[236] I agree with this but believe that it is important to be aware of ones own epistemological assumptions underlying ones use of a specific research method. Are certain methods, and approaches to those methods, more appropriate to a postfoundationalist perspective? Mason agrees with the need to appreciate both the importance of both methodological perspectives but notes a vital caution as to the diversity within each broad approach itself:

> I do not think research practice has to involve stark either/or choices between qualitative and quantitative methodology. Partly, this is because neither "quantitative" nor "qualitative" bodies of philosophy method and technique which they are sometimes seen to be. This means that any researcher should always think carefully about integrating different methods.[237]

The researcher believes that perhaps the "mixed methods" approach to research that Osmer refers to is best.[238]

Qualitative Research

Here, an attempt is made to view the situation from the perspective of those who are being studied, and to get to grips with the social context being discussed.[239] There is an attempt to interpret and understand a given context in complexity and detail:

> Qualitative researchers, wishing to focus on the worldviews of the subjects under study, tend to operate with an open and flexible research strategy rather than one which is overly prescriptive from the start. This means that research problems tend to be organized around more general and open questions rather than tightly defined and theory-driven questions. Qualitative researchers tend to favour a process that formulates and tests theories and concepts as they arise from within the data under collection.[240]

---

236. Dreyer, "Practical Theology in SA," 3.
237. Mason, *Qualitative Researching*, 4.
238. Osmer, *Practical Theology*, 50.
239. Cartledge, *Practical Theology*, 68.
240. Mason, *Qualitative Researching*, 70.

There is a wide range of approaches to qualitative research which makes it difficult and slippery to define.[241] Osmer lists six different strategies to conduct qualitative research: life history/narrative research, case studies, ethnographic research, grounded theory research, phenomenological research, and advocacy research.[242] In terms of actually generating the data as part of the various strategies Mason lists people, organizations, texts, specific settings, objects/artifacts, and events that might take place.[243]

Qualitative methodology often requires that researchers immerse themselves within the group/person/environment being studied. Cartledge describes this process of enmeshing within the group as "participant observation."[244] This might require different levels of participation or non-participation from those involved. The interviews that participant observers conduct are often conducted in an ad hoc manner. It is also regarded as unavoidable that the researchers have some influence on the social dynamic of their study, regardless of the level in which they participate.[245] The interviewing that takes place is often unstructured by nature and allows for deeper interaction between the interviewer and interviewee.[246] This is not entirely true as no form of interview is totally devoid of structure.[247] These participatory observation stories provide information on "insider perspectives and their practices."[248]

Focus groups that take into account life histories, oral histories, and documentary analysis can also be used.[249] Hendriks notes that, as qualitative research is of a more philosophical nature, its expression remains less formalized and more flexible in its research design.[250] Here, the contention is that this points to a research methodology that would be more suited to the less academically orientated person—which would represent most who attend our churches. Heitink would probably equate qualitative research with what he discusses as "explorative research," which is "more intuitive

---

241. Swinton and Mowat, *Practical Theology*, 29.
242. Osmer, *Practical Theology*, 50–53.
243. Mason, *Qualitative Researching*, 52.
244. Cartledge, *Practical Theology*, 70.
245. Ibid., 71.
246. Ibid., 72.
247. Mason, *Qualitative Researching*, 62.
248. Mouton, *How to Succeed*, 148.
249. Cartledge, *Practical Theology*, 72.
250. Hendriks, *Studying Congregations in Africa*, 226.

A Postfoundationalist Practical Theology

than methodical. The result is therefore limited to preliminary statements, models, or search strategies, for which one can adduce solid arguments."[251]

Another form of qualitative research is that of participatory action research, which Mouton describes in the following manner:

> Studies that involve the subjects of research (research participants) as integral to part of the design. [They] use mainly qualitative methods in order to gain understanding and insight into lifeworlds of research participants. Most types of PAR have an explicit (political) commitment to the empowerment of participants and to changing the social conditions of the participants.[252]

Cameron et al.'s book *Talking about God in Practice: Theological Action research and Practical Theology* make a strong case for action research.[253] The authors claim that it is the first time action research has emerged within practical theology. This is not entirely true. Hendriks proposed this form of research when discussing his research paradigms.[254] Important for action research is that it is context-based, collaborative between researchers and participants, emphasizes diversity, that meanings arise from the process that lead to action and those actions to new meanings.[255] This is the research paradigm that Hendriks proposes for faith-based organizations.[256] To my mind, the participatory action research and the participant observation research are vital when calling for a practical theology that is local and seeks to take into account the experience of real people. These experiences often go beyond the bounds of practice or action as "Many experiences—such as being touched by a specific atmosphere, being opened to a disclosure experience, being caught by 'flow' experiences and other religious or cultural phenomena—reach beyond the category of practice."[257]

I believe that one would be hard pressed to really understand any given local context without some form of qualitative research. And if a postfoundationalist approach values understanding one's local context as a source of knowledge, then qualitative research is critical.

---

251. Heitink, *Practical Theology*, 230.
252. Mouton, *How to Succeed*, 150.
253. Cameron et al. *Talking about God in Practice*, 39.
254. Hendriks, *Studying Congregations in Africa*, 216–17.
255. Cameron et al., *Talking about God in Practice*, 36.
256. Hendriks, *Studying Congregations in Africa*, 219.
257. Heimbrock, "From Data to Theory," 290.

Postfoundationalist Reflections in Practical Theology

Quantitative Research

This form of research, of course, has been most prevalent in the natural sciences where measurements, control, variables, and experiments come into play.[258] Traditionally it found expression with positivistic approaches in the natural sciences but eventually spread to the social and human sciences.[259] Neuman believes that quantitative research still relies heavily on positivistic assumptions.[260] Baranov has shown that positivism itself has morphed in a variety of ways from embryonic positivism, logical positivism, and post positivism. Baranov believes that the present position is the realisation that the quest of positivism, originating with Descartes, for absolute certainty is an impossibility. Knowledge is still attainable and there is progress in human understanding but certainty is not possible.[261] Objectivity, though, is still prized even if certainty cannot be achieved. Johnson and Christenson explain:

> Quantitative researchers attempt to operate under the assumption of objectivity. They assume that there is a reality to be observed and that rational observers who look at the same phenomenon will basically agree on its existence and characteristics. They try to remain as neutral and value free as they can, and they try to avoid human bias whenever possible. In a sense, quantitative researchers attempt to study the phenomena that are of interest to them "from a distance."[262]

It is a form of research that is far from simple and involves the use of statistical and numerical data[263] using a language of "variables, hypotheses, units of analysis and causal explanations."[264] This form of research is "highly formalised as well as more explicitly controlled."[265] It has often been viewed as the best type of research, as Cartledge explains, "It has been usual to regard quantitative researchers as embracing the more scientific or factual ap-

---

258. Cartledge, *Practical Theology*, 74.
259. Baranov, *Conceptual Foundations*, 78.
260. Neuman, *Social Research Methods*, 96.
261. Baranov, *Conceptual Foundations*, 74–75.
262. Johnson and Christensen, *Educational Research*, 36.
263. Heitink, *Practical Theology*, 229; Johnson and Christensen, *Educational Research*, 33.
264. Neuman, *Social Research Methods*, 96.
265. Hendriks, *Studying Congregations in Africa*, 226.

proach, while qualitative researchers are regarded as embracing approaches that are more person centerd and have more in common with the arts."[266]

Many prefer this method of research as qualitative methods are often time consuming, and practical theologians like Astley[267] consider it to be more reliable and valid. Often though there is a loss in "richness and meaning."[268] Like qualitative research there is a variety of different approaches to quantitative research but broadly fall into the two categories of experimental and non-experimental research.[269] My intention here is not to give a detailed discussion of the various options for quantitative research. My intention is to give enough information to be able to distinguish the two options and make some remarks with regard to foundationalism. To that we now turn.

Qualitative or Quantitative Research?

Both forms of research have their strengths and weaknesses and both should be incorporated into practical theology in terms of how they explain and describe the raw material that forms part of one's theological reflection. In terms of understanding the glocal nature of a specific group or person, quantitative data can be of immense value; this is specifically so with regard to global issues. In the work of the sociologist, Manuel Castells, one can see the importance of good quantitative research for explaining the vast global currents that sweep through our world. The difficulty is that the average person will find this form of theological reflection difficult, which is why qualitative research proves to be a better vehicle for research that takes place locally.

The nature of the qualitative method of research is also more geared to a deeper understanding of the experience that arises from communities and individuals who can form the starting point of theological reflection, as Cartledge explains: "Qualitative research does not present its findings as 'true' but as an invitation to view things from a particular perspective. It aims to enable the search for meaning in a complex social world."[270]

---

266. Cartledge, *Practical Theology*, 74.
267. Astley, *Ordinary Theology*, 98.
268. Babbie, *The Practice of Social Research*, 26.
269. Johnson and Christensen, *Educational Research*, 41–47.
270. Cartledge, *Practical Theology*, 78.

Qualitative research is also not a *fleeting* engagement with those being studied but rather a sustained engagement.[271]

The ability for those who are unable to do good quantitative research to come to grips with the global realities that form part of theological reflection would mean they would need to have access to various quantitative data that would help them understand what effects global realities have on their local context. Still, a mixed methods approach[272] might be the preferred option in trying to understand the reality of a given context. With the rejection of a positivistic approach to reality, and the demise of a foundationalist quest for certainty, a mixed methods approach could in fact provide a more reliable picture of the reality concerned. Johnson and Christensen noted that theirs was a time when the mixing of qualitative and quantitative approaches was seen as impossible and was known as the "incompatability thesis."[273] This mixed approach has much to offer for a:

> Creative and thoughtful mixing of assumptions, ideas, and methods can be very helpful and offers a thirds paradigm. The mixing of ideas and approaches has been present throughout history because mixing or combining builds upon what we know and offers new ways to study our world.... Mixed research offers an exciting way of conducting educational research.[274]

Cartledge calls for the importance of both qualitative and quantitative research for practical theology where one, "will recognize the value of engagement with the lifeworld of the people under study as well as the value of a more detached and structured approach that uses the mechanisms of distance. Therefore knowledge is to be gained both by participation and by reflection, by engagement and detachment."[275] I believe that mixed research approach would be one way toward getting a more *thick* description of a given local context. It honors a critical realist understanding of reality that does not embrace a positivistic certainty but also believes that one can gain understanding of that reality. Any approach that deems itself as the only way to acquire knowledge has fallen prey to foundationalist assumptions— whether qualitative or quantitative. I still hold that it would be enormously difficult to have a good understanding of a local context without qualitative

---

271. Ibid., 81.
272. Osmer, *Practical Theology*, 50.
273. Johnson and Christensen, *Educational Research*, 31.
274. Ibid.
275. Cartledge, *Practical Theology*, 82.

means. It is perhaps best suited to understanding "individuals, groups and communities in depth."[276]

An Experiential, Global, and Social Scientific Approach to a Postfoundationalist Practical Theology?

The previous few sections have been exploring a glocal praxis-based approach to practical theology. It has explored the *pastoral concern* dynamic of what is known as the *pastoral cycle* and has also argued that praxis takes place between the tension of practice and theory. More specifically, the local dimension of practical theology, from which the pastoral concern emerges, has been examined. The argument was that theological reflection emerges from experience, which is a source for practical theological reflection consistent with postfoundationalism. It was mentioned that in order to understand the *local experience* means one ought to take global factors and currents into account—hence a glocal practical theology. Lastly it was stated that in order to understand this glocal experience one must critically use and engage the social sciences in terms of gathering the *raw data* that will be taken up into further dialogue with the culture's resources and with the Christian story (represented by tradition and Scripture). To this part of the pastoral cycle we now turn.

A CORRELATIONAL HERMENEUTIC

Pastoral Reflection

What we have looked at so far is the first part of the pastoral cycle, and that of beginning with a pastoral concern, consistent with a postfoundationalist approach. The pastoral concern seeks to take the glocal nature of any given reality into account. It also seeks to value and understand people's experience as a source for theological reflection. In attempting to do this, it embraces the social sciences, realising its potential pitfalls and limitations, to provide insight into the nature of any given pastoral concern. A pastoral concern can range from understanding poverty in one's local community to the crisis of pollution in one's local area. It has individual, corporate and ecological dimensions, consistent with a missional practical theology.

---

276. Osmer, *Practical Theology*, 50.

Postfoundationalist Reflections in Practical Theology

The second step is to bring this *raw material* into a dialectical dialogue with cultural resources on the one hand, and the Christian classics on the other. Here again, we find a role for the human sciences, but also the natural sciences, according to the specific pastoral concern chosen. Dealing with ecological concerns could involve the use of biology, geography and science as a resource for reflection. Dealing with a given individual's crisis could call for the insights of psychology, or psychology of religion.[277] Politics, economics and philosophy could play a role in other areas. Of late, Wolfteich[278] has demonstrated the importance of the discipline of Spirituality as a potential dialogue partner. Depending on the nature of the pastoral concern, it will lead to the correct appropriation of any given natural, human or other science. This engagement with other disciplines is one of the crucial aspects for a postfoundationalist approach as noted by van Huyssteen.

On the other side of the correlational hermeneutic, we bring the *raw material* of the pastoral concern into dialogue with the Christian classics. Here with the Christian classics, I believe Stanley Grenz's call for theology, and specifically *evangelical theology*, to move beyond foundationalism is vital. This involves both the church's tradition, as well as the use of Scripture. Needless to say, the importance of the traditional biblical disciplines of biblical studies, church history, systematic theology, and theological ethics becomes obvious. As already noted, this has been one of the weaker aspects within practical theology. In dealing with both the cultural and the Christian sources we must take into account an epistemological shift that, in turn, must lead us to a postfoundationalist approach to sources within practical theology consistent with our earlier discussions. This theoretical moment of pastoral reflection must result in a theoretical proposal for pastoral action that must then move back to practice in the form of an intervention in the real world.[279]

In dealing with pastoral reflection, we shall examine the nature of the correlational hermeneutic itself, followed by an understanding of what a postfoundationalist approach should imply for this hermeneutic in respect of Scripture. Then, more specifically, both the role of the human sciences and the Christian classics will be examined.

---

277. Ganzevoort, "Strange Bedfellows."
278. Wolfteich, "Animating Questions," 123.
279. De Kock, "Open Seminary at Tabor," 9.

A Postfoundationalist Practical Theology

A Critical Correlational Hermeneutic

The correlational hermeneutic finds itself as a movement within the second part of the pastoral cycle, which we called *pastoral reflection*. We have already noted the importance of the critical correlational hermeneutic for our discussion of a postfoundationalist approach to practical theology and theology in general. "In theological reflection then, a postmodern critique of foundationalist assumptions will therefore be an inextricable part of a postfoundationalist model of rationality, and will definitely shape the way in which theology is located within the context of interdisciplinary reflection."[280]

Poling and Miller's discussion of the correlational hermeneutic shows the three ways in which the correlational hermeneutic could be worked out. Ranging from one that promotes the importance of the human sciences on the one hand, called the *critical scientific approach* to, on the other hand, the *critical confessional approach* that pushes for the prominence of the Christian tradition. In the middle is the *critical correlational approach*, which seeks to hold the two in tension and allow for mutual change and engagement. The *transversal approach* proposed by van Huyssteen seeks not so much to hold them in tension, as to see the points of overlap between disciplines relevant to the given contextual discussion or situation.

Of course, there is a wide variety of correlational approaches—one might even say a bewildering variety. Ballard and Pritchard note three of these.[281] The first is a dialogue between the situation on the one hand, and the theological tradition on the other. A second option is one that seeks to bring pastoral concerns together with ethics. The public nature of this subset of the correlational hermeneutic comes to the fore here.[282] The third option is the hermeneutical one where an attempt to interpret biblical stories and one's situation are important.

Tillich is the most well-known proponent of the correlational hermeneutic, which is often considered his most enduring contribution to modern theology.[283] His correlational perspective involves a dialogue with psychology, and Christian tradition on the other.[284] More recent exponents

---

280. van Huyssteen, *Essays in Postfoundationalist Theology*, 13.
281. Ballard and Pritchard, *Practical Theology in Action*, 64–68.
282. van Huyssteen, *Essays in Postfoundationalist Theology*, 66.
283. Grenz and Olson, *Twentieth Century Theology*, 119.
284. Graham et al., *Theological Reflection*, 155.

Postfoundationalist Reflections in Practical Theology

are Tracy and Browning. Tracy argues for a revised critical correlational method and one that seeks for an interface between cultural concerns and theological truth claims.[285] Browning, who leans heavily on Tracy, tries to connect two poles, which he believes have often been split up. "These two poles are the confessional approach (which sees theology as primarily witnessing to the narrative structure of faith) and the apologetic approach (which defends the rationality of the faith and tries to increase its plausibility to the contemporary secular mind)."[286] Browning, like Tracy, views theology as a dialogue between the Christian message and contemporary cultural experiences and practices.[287]

I am aware that people mean very different things when discussing a correlational hermeneutic. The form of correlational hermeneutic I adhere to certainly takes, at its base element, the assumption of its dialogical nature in terms of how various perspectives interact and correlate with each other.[288]

Here, the argument will be for a correlational hermeneutic that seeks to hold both sources (human sciences and Christian tradition) in creative tension. It gives neither primacy nor dominance to either in the discussion. It is a *critical* dialogue in that each side opens itself up to potential revision or change. It does not believe that each discipline is locked in its own world, unable to *speak* to, or with, each other. The resources of rationality shared by all disciplines enable a transversal approach, where different disciplines work together to solve common and complex problems shared by both. This is in line with a postfoundationalist approach.

Once the pastoral concern (that has arisen out of local experience) comes to the surface, it meets further sources for reflection in the human sciences and the Christian classics. In this moment, a threefold dialogue emerges with relevant insights that interact with each other in plotting a way forward for action. As mentioned earlier, the specific resources used depend on the nature of the pastoral concern. At this point, a specific example will help illustrate how the correlational hermeneutic works out in practice.

A young women in a large urban evangelical church is confronted with the alienating experience of being gifted in leadership, but is told

---

285. Tracy, *The Analogical Imagination*, 64.
286. Browning, *A Fundamental Practical Theology*, 44.
287. Ibid., 46.
288. Hendriks, *Studying Congregations in Africa*, 21.

that her denomination does not allow her to hold certain leadership positions. The pastoral concern is the crisis of this woman's experience and the conflict between her personal experience (being a gifted women) and her experience of being in a faith community that does not allow her experience to be valid. She then takes up these concerns in a dialogue with the Christian classics and the human sciences. Within church tradition and the Scriptures she finds a largely patriarchal view of women's role in church. However, she also finds a different strand within church tradition (both past and present) and within Scripture, which seems to allow for a fuller expression of women's leadership giftings.

When listening to the voices of the human sciences, she becomes aware of the sociological barriers that have held women back. She comes across psychological studies that demonstrate that women have equal ability to lead as men. As she holds these various sources in tension, she is able to discern a way forward. The correlational hermeneutic, as the researcher understands it, is that place of tension as her experience is taken into dialogue with the two poles of the human sciences and the Christian classics. An attempt to examine and delineate what is understood by the human sciences and the Christian classics will follow.

The Human Sciences

We have already examined the human sciences or, more specifically, the social sciences, when discussing experience as our starting point for theological reflection. One ought to be equally vigilant when heeding the human sciences as part of a correlational hermeneutic.

The challenge we face here is one that illustrates the particular *torment* of being a practical theologian. For, depending on the pastoral concern that one is dealing with, it will have an influence over a variety of sciences that might come into play. This problem is even more apparent in the light of how we defined the missional nature of practical theology. If we say that anything and everything can come under the orbit of practical theology, then we say that practical theology has the potential to touch any dynamic and situation in life. We also know that the human sciences touch different dimensions of our lives in a variety of contexts and are, therefore, vital in any form of missional practical theology.

When discussing the nature of practical theology in the first half of this book, we noted the fact that a practical theologian might be called a jack of all trades. Firet comments on the fact that if practical theologians seek to do a thorough job, they might have to specialize in a host of different disciplines. It becomes even more challenging if we hope for a form of theological reflection that most people would be able to achieve. Yet, if we argue for a correlational hermeneutic, at least in the way that I understand it, we are bound to come into contact with a host of different sciences. Therefore, practical theology must take an interdisciplinary approach seriously—again, important for a truly postfoundational theology.[289] This is even at the risk of being seen in a negative light as Ballard and Pritchard explain:

> Interdisciplinary dialogue has become a necessity. Moreover it is recognized that creative insights often come precisely at those places where disciplines overlap and challenge each other. There is, therefore, no need to be ashamed to be living at the boundaries, in however a lowly way. Maybe the practical theologian has to endure the risk of marginalization, ridicule and error, but he or she can also be at the place of the new possibility, discovery and prophecy.[290]

Firet comments that practical theology will often have to use the aid of its sister disciplines and various other sciences.[291] Of necessity, this will mean that it will have to rely on secondary sources more than might be desirable.[292] It will also pose a challenge as to which disciplines are chosen with which to engage.[293] Ganzevoort has argued for a social constructivist approach to practical theology as a way of creating this dialogue between practical theology and other disciplines. He believes this to be vital for a public theology that is taken seriously by the social sciences.

> The language we use depends on the criteria that are important to the discourse at hand. In the realm of the church, one may employ religious language more easily. Dealing with social scientists we will accommodate our language to include their language and theories. This is not a matter of chameleonic adaptation, but a consequence of understanding that the meaning of the term is located in a conversation. Obviously, if we are to engage in such

289. van Huyssteen, *Essays in Postfoundationalist Theology*, 13.
290. Ballard and Pritchard, *Practical Theology in Action*, 115.
291. Firet, *Dynamics in Pastoring*, 10.
292. Ballard and Pritchard, *Practical Theology in Action*, 116.
293. Graham et al., *Theological Reflection*, 167.

A Postfoundationalist Practical Theology

diverse conversations, we will encounter conflicts of interpretation that we cannot accommodate. The practical theologian in that case faces the difficult task of maintaining his or her professional integrity while working in conflicting languages.[294]

Although it is true that the social sciences tend to dominate in practical theology, there must be a place for the other human sciences—or any science for that matter. As already discussed, the implications for this means that depending on the pastoral concern of any given moment, a specific science or a combination of sciences could come into dialogue correlationally with the Christian classics. In reflecting on the emotional abuse of a child, there would be a role for psychology. When trying to understand the destitute situation of a given family, economic insights could prove vital. Sociology, history, philosophy, biology, political science, medicine, law, or developmental studies—anything could become a partner in dialogue. Sanchez has argued for the importance of this interdisciplinary thinking, what he calls a transdisciplinary approach, for understanding the concrete realities within Puerto Rican society.[295] Pattison reminds us that "interdisciplinary work is notoriously difficult to do" but "is the most incredibly rewarding work possible."[296]

Despite this, one must be cautious to remember that the human sciences, in and of themselves, are not neutral. They have also been affected by the postmodern critique of knowledge and the epistemological shift beyond foundationalism that we have already explored.

Foundationalism and the Human Sciences

We mentioned Descartes and Locke as the genesis of foundationalism—the idea that we can come to certain knowledge by finding a sure footing or foundation on which to construct our views. Locke is of specific relevance when we examine the foundationalist setting of the human sciences. Grenz argues that Locke seeks to find a universal method of enquiry that could be applicable to all disciplines:

> Locke argued that the foundation for demonstrative knowledge, characterized by universality and certainty, and which can be

---

294. Ganzevoort, "The Social Construction of Revelation," 3–4.
295. Sánchez, "The Emerging Field," 230–31.
296. Pattison, *The Challenge of Practical Theology*, 21.

stated in the form of assertions, lies in sense experience, i.e. observations of the world, from which we abstract ideas and induce conclusions. His proposal, known as empiricism, provided the methodological foundationalist turn in science.[297]

Whether starting with an empirical foundation with Locke, or a rationalist one with Descartes, this reigning paradigm found its home in many of the human sciences that emerged from the Enlightenment. The universal claim of science, which emerged from this paradigm, was brought into question in the twentieth century. Positivism, with its innate foundationalism, was itself called into question.[298] It was Karl Popper who led the attack on both the rationalists and empiricists. He pointed out that both sides regard their basic truths as self-evident and immediately certain. For Popper according to Küng our knowledge always begins with "conjectures, assumptions, patterns, hypotheses, which must be exposed to scrutiny."[299] Popper proposes that we cannot therefore achieve knowledge by verification but only through falsification. Popper's falsification theory proved to be provisional, and as Küng notes, "his falsification theory has been exposed to falsification and has in fact been falsified."[300]

Despite Popper "killing" positivism and pulling out the carpet from underneath foundationalism in science, it was left to Thomas Kuhn to chart a way forward with his paradigm theory. Bosch explains:

> The paradigm theory implies a fundamental break with preceding theories of science, particularly logical positivism's emphasis on verification as well as Karl Popper's idea of "falsification" as sure ways in which scientific research advances. It is widely accepted today, in all the sciences (natural as well as social) that total objectivity is an illusion, and that knowledge belongs to a community and is influenced by the dynamics operative in such a community. This means that not only scientific data are tested, but also the researchers themselves.[301]

Kuhn's basic thesis is that science and knowledge advance not by progressive steps, but rather through revolutions. A revolution takes place as a reigning paradigm is slowly called into question by a network of diverse

---

297. Grenz, *Renewing the Center*, 222.
298. Küng, *Does God Exist?*, 102.
299. Ibid., 103.
300. Ibid., 106.
301. Bosch, *Transforming Mission*, 185.

A Postfoundationalist Practical Theology

social and scientific factors.[302] The knowledge community begins to realize the shortcomings of its paradigm and realizes that traditional answers cannot solve the new questions. As one shifts into the new paradigm, you begin to see the same objects, with the same instruments, in a different manner.[303] The consequence of seeing knowledge as a series of paradigm shifts calls into question any form of objective truth. We are left rather with something that is relatively objective.[304]

Bosch argues that Kuhn's understanding has direct relevance for all disciplines. Not only does it help us move beyond the Enlightenment's foundationalism, but actually helps us to understand the very paradigm change that all the human sciences find themselves in today—which, of course, is the dissolution of the Enlightenment paradigm itself.[305]

A brief attempt was made to show how science has moved beyond foundationalism and it was stated that the positivist foundationalism that emerged out of the Enlightenment has given way to a nonfoundationalist perspective, exemplified by Popper, and more definitively by Kuhn.

In understanding the nonfoundationalism of the human sciences, we are also forced to come to grips with Jurgen Habermas's relativizing of knowledge, which Küng describes as "social-critical de-ideologizing."[306] Before discussing Habermas, the work of Hans-Georg Gadamer must be noted. He is important in demonstrating that our tradition and horizon of meaning has an impact on how texts and reality are understood.[307] There is a mediating between our present horizon and meaning, and the text's present horizon of meaning.[308] Heitink describes Gadamar's position in the following manner, "In our attempts to understand texts or reality we all operate with our own biases. Understanding is always conditioned by the context of the one who explains. . . . Objective knowledge does not exist."[309]

Gadamer proposes a hermeneutical approach in helping us to gain understanding.[310] Habermas critiques Gadamer in not paying more attention

---

302. Ibid., 184.
303. Küng, *Does God Exist?*, 109.
304. Ibid., 110.
305. Bosch, *Transforming Mission*, 185.
306. Küng, *Does God Exist?*, 110.
307. Heitink, *Practical Theology*, 185.
308. Baronov, *Conceptual Foundations*, 125.
309. Heitink, *Practical Theology*, 184.
310. Ibid.

to the role of ideology and power.[311] Habermas proposes a community in dialogue approach to arrive at knowledge that can lead to ethical decision-making in society.[312] Browning notes that many of Habermas's critics have accused him of a foundationalist drive, and even see him as a continuation of the Enlightenment quest for certainty.[313] This is not the place for a sustained interaction and delineation of the views of Habermas or Gadamer. What was intended was to show that with both of them (and Paul Ricoeur) a shift to a more social interpretive process in terms of how knowledge is gained has been seen.[314] Bosch shows the connection between these social theorists and that of Polyani and Kuhn:

> In spite of the differences between them, it could be argued that there is a degree of convergence between the theories expounded by Kuhn and those espoused by Polyani. Habermas, Paul Ricoeur, and more recently John Thompson and Charles Taylor, have worked out similar ideas. In all these views scientific theory, history, sociology, and hermeneutics go hand in hand. A new vision is emerging, and it affects all the sciences, both human and natural.[315]

My basic thesis regarding the use of the various sciences in practical theology has been that it ought to be conducted in light of the postfoundationalist turn, while taking into account the critique of reason and knowledge that the Enlightenment held dear. The previous discussion in showing how there has been a shift in science and the theory of knowledge, has direct bearing on how one engages with the sciences as part of a critical correlational hermeneutic and transversal approach. Browning certainly believes that the results of the hermeneutical turn (represented by Gadamer, Habermas, and Ricoeur) are of direct relevance for a responsible use of the human sciences in practical theology.[316]

Browning has shown that the consequences of Gadamer's understanding of dialogue mean that any human science ought to acknowledge its historical situatedness.[317] This again, is consistent with a postfoundational

---

311. Ibid., 186.
312. Van Gelder, "Mission," 133.
313. Browning, *A Fundamental Practical Theology*, 69.
314. Van Gelder, *The Ministry*, 109.
315. Bosch, *Transforming Mission*, 351.
316. Browning, *A Fundamental Practical Theology*, 79.
317. Ibid., 81.

approach, yet as van Huyssteen has shown does not impede a transversal approach to interdisciplinary engagement. Due to each discipline's situatedness, any appropriation of the human sciences must come to terms with the implicit values and presuppositions that accompany the discipline. This applies not only to the discipline in question, but to the researcher who conducts research within any discipline. Browning further notes that what emerges from these considerations is that the hidden values and assumptions are essentially religious. He comments that:

> If the social and human sciences are rooted in a tradition, if that tradition inevitably influences their interpretive perspectives (their pre-understanding and prejudices), and if that tradition has religious dimensions, does it follow that the interpretive horizon of the social sciences is coloured by the religio-cultural backgrounds of the researchers?[318]

Engaging with the Human Sciences

When listening to the human sciences, in light of what we have already discussed, we can make some tentative conclusions. The first is that a correlational hermeneutic cannot do without the human sciences, as it is vital in terms of shedding light on any given pastoral concern that is subject to theological reflection. Secondly, that this requires a transversal interdisciplinary approach that seeks to build bridges with others. Thirdly, practical theologians should be aware of their own bias in terms of the material they select. By this is meant that when there are differing perspectives in a given human science, an endeavor to listen to both sides as part of the dialogue should be attempted. Fourthly, due to accepting a postfoundationalist approach to the human sciences, one must accept the provisional nature of the conclusions and perspectives on offer. Lastly, and related to the previous point, it is recognized that the human sciences retain their own prejudice, bias, and ideological coloring. This affects the discipline as a whole, as well as the unique individual researchers. The religious dimension of the human sciences makes us aware of uncritically accepting their findings, while downplaying the contribution of the Christian classics.

In practice, the task of listening to the various contributions will prove to be difficult—if not impossible. Ballard and Pritchard suggest an attempt

---

318. Browning, *A Fundamental Practical Theology*, 89.

to gain some form of specialization in at least two human sciences and to try to stay up-to-date with their developments.[319] For the majority who embrace the task of theological reflection, this remains an idealistic illusion. Rather, having access to a good resource base of secondary sources will be the most likely option.

In all probability, to engage with the human sciences will prove to be the more difficult part of the correlational hermeneutic. This is due to the fact that most often those who engage in theological reflection and practical theology are already familiar, even if in a very limited sense, with the Christian classics. We now turn to a consideration of this second pole of the correlational hermeneutic.

The Christian Classics

The Christian classics are represented by both the Christian Scriptures and the church's tradition. They are of the utmost importance for practical theology as Cartledge notes:

> It is essential that practical theologians engage with scripture and Tradition in a rigorous way in order to understand the divine revelation and how it has been used historically. The Christian metanarrative of Scripture as inspiration and truthful vision provides an essential critique with respect to the focus of study, and without which it might become a form of religious studies.[320]

Of course, the understanding and appropriation of these sources to any given pastoral concern is no easy task. The subjective nature of one's selection with regard to the content of these sources is inescapable. Which resources does one consult? Which Scriptures? Whose interpretation of Scripture? Whose tradition? We propose that the practical theologian ought to try to bring into account as many diverse perspectives as is possible and realistic. This is what we would call *the ecumenical nature of practical theology*. Recently Hastings has argued for just such an approach for practical theology in what he calls a "Missional-Ecumenical Model."[321] It remains suspicious of one's own confessional starting point and must allow itself to remain

---

319. Ballard and Pritchard, *Practical Theology in Action*, 116.
320. Cartledge, *Affective Theological Practice*, 39.
321. Hastings, *Practical Theology*.

A Postfoundationalist Practical Theology

open to critical revision from within the broader faith community. This is of vital importance in the responsible use of Christian resources.

This can be demonstrated by going back to our earlier example of the woman who was denied leadership responsibility on the basis of her gender. If the only Christian resources consulted are those of a narrow segment of the evangelical community, she would find her personal experience of being a gifted woman invalidated. Her experience would then need serious revision in terms of how she understands her role as a woman within the church. If she utilized the specific understanding of the Scriptures by certain evangelicals from within the Southern Baptist tradition in the United States, she would have been left with the following *voice* from the pole of Christian classics that says the following: "[T]he Bible teaches that men and women fulfil different roles in relation to each other, charging man with a unique leadership role, it bases this differentiation not on temporary cultural norms but on permanent facts of creation."[322]

If, however, in her utilization of Scripture and tradition, she exposed herself to a different segment within the evangelical tradition who held a different understanding of Scripture, she might conclude differently that: "Gender, in and of itself, neither privileges nor curtails one's ability to be used to advance God's kingdom or to glorify God in any dimension of ministry, mission, society and family. The differences between men and women do not justify granting men unique and perpetual prerogatives of leadership and authority not shared by women."[323] Responsible use of the Christian classics would seek to listen to the divergent voices from within the tradition. It would seek to hear what the Methodists, Catholics, Anglicans, or Orthodox would say regarding the role of women in its history and dogma. It would seek to see how various approaches to Scripture and its interpretations yield different views on the role of women within the church. What have the liberal voices said? How do evangelicals understand the Scriptures? This ecumenical approach to the Christian classics honors the Christian tradition in its many forms and seeks to bring different perspectives into dialogue with one another. Again, it is important to remind ourselves that these resources are not being utilized in some distant abstract academic setting. They are being appropriated to a unique pastoral concern arising out of real people's reality and experience. In fact, many women's experiences in the past have given rise to fresh reflection within various

---

322. Piper, "A Vision," 135.
323. Pierce et al., *Discovering Biblical Equality*, 13.

traditions, as well as a fresh examination of the Scriptures. These reflections then become a further resource for new experiences into the future as new pastoral concerns arise.

The Scriptures

Graham et al.[324] noted that theological reflection on traditional Christian sources has been weak. They define practical theology's relationship with the study of the bible as *uneasy*. Ballard believes that the use of scripture in practical theology has in fact "proven elusive and problematic."[325] Its importance must be reclaimed.

As the sacred book of the Christian community, the Scriptures are a source for theological reflection. Many would claim it to be the *only* source and norm for Christian theology. Others would not only claim it to be the only source for theological reflection, but indeed propose a specific view of Scripture that ought to be normative. Here, Scripture is seen to be inerrant—without error. A collection of "immutable laws and infallible truths."[326] Of course, if this were true, there would be no need for the human sciences to be part of the discussion. Nor would there be any need for one's unique local experience to be taken into account. Then, all we would need would be an applied theology. In a foundationalist sense, Scripture now becomes the foundation from which all other knowledge derives, and is based upon. This is what one of the stalwarts of the evangelical movement proposed, "The issue is clear: is the Bible truth and without error wherever it speaks, including where it touches history and the cosmos, or is it only in some revelational sense where it touches religious subjects?"[327]

Of course, like many evangelicals, Schaeffer would argue that the Scriptures must be without error. Within evangelicalism itself, however, there has been a rethinking with regard to one's view of Scripture. Millard Erickson, who himself believes in inerrancy, has sought to warn those within the evangelical movement about this rethinking.[328] Others, such as Olson,[329] have urged the identity-forming nature of Scripture for the Chris-

---

324. Graham et al., *Theological Reflection*, 7.
325. Ballard, "The Use of Scripture," 163.
326. Hanson, *The People Called*, 535.
327. Schaefer, "No Final Conflict," 121.
328. Erickson, *The Evangelical Left*, 76–78.
329. Olson, *The Mosaic of Christian Belief*, 67.

A Postfoundationalist Practical Theology

tian community and prefer the term "inspiration." At this point, it must suffice to say that I do not believe that a critical correlational approach to practical theology can be possible with a doctrine of Scripture that claims to be without error. It would make nonsense of the use of the human sciences (except perhaps to confirm revelation) and would seriously diminish the power of experience as a starting point. It would also require a return to a pre-1960s approach to practical theology that would champion a foundationalist and applied theology.

The desire to see the Bible as inerrant is actually an outworking of the modernist and foundationalist agenda that we discussed earlier. Stanley Grenz shows convincingly that the Princeton theologians, who spearheaded the inerrancy debate, were heavily influenced by Enlightenment foundationalist rationalism.[330] This was an attempt to find a sure foundation for the theological truths that emerged from the Bible. It rested on an assumption that knowledge requires that the human senses can perceive the world as it actually is. Foundationalism has had an enormous influence on evangelicalism and its approach to Scripture:

> The firm foundation the hymn writer believed had been laid in God's excellent word came to equated with the words in the Bible themselves, the veracity of which was thought to be unimpeachable when measured by the canons of human reason. With such an incontrovertible foundation in place, conservative theologians were confident that they would deduce from Scripture the great theological truths that lay within its pages.... Enlightenment foundationalism seeped into neo-evangelical theology and became its reigning paradigm.[331]

A Nonfoundationalist Approach to Scripture?

If we are serious about moving beyond foundationalism in practical theology, an appropriate way to engage with the Christian Scriptures as a source will be needed. This is of critical importance for a postfoundationalist approach, because as Ganzevoort notes, "there are of course strands of practical theology in which a straightforward reference to revelation is accepted, often resulting in deductive or foundationalist approaches."[332] If Scripture

---

330. Grenz, *Renewing the Center*, 70.
331. Ibid., 189–90.
332. Ganzevoort, "The Social Construction of Revelation," 1.

is not inerrant, and the sure foundation for knowledge, then how do we appropriate its insights?

With Humility

A chastened rationality means that no matter how certain we think our interpretation of Scripture is we remain finite human beings. Our prior confessional and ideological commitments that weigh in upon our interpretation can easily cloud our judgement. Being aware of our own frailty, might not give us the right answer, but it certainly places us in the correct posture to be open to further insights and guard against potential bias. We agree with Wright that we cannot "read the text straight"[333] in a naïve realistic manner. Along with realizing our confessional and ideological bias, one will need to be aware of one's personal and historical location that affects how one approaches Scripture. Heitink puts it in the following way:

> One must first of all acknowledge the bias, or the prejudicing, determined by historical, sociological, and historical factors. How people understand the words of Scripture and apply these in a concrete situation is in part determined by their historical context, by the *WirKüngsgeschichte* of traditions within the group to which they belong, and by their personality, their possibilities for understanding, their personal history, with psychological factors that may either foster or hinder religious understanding.[334]

A practical theological engagement with Scripture then approaches the text with due awareness of its own bias. It also realizes that a *chastened rationality* requires that it remains suspicious of simple readings, as well as obvious conclusions.

Ecumenically

This is essentially related to a humble appropriation of Scripture. Instead of claiming that one specific confessional approach has a monopoly on understanding what Scripture teaches, we in fact affirm the opposite. It involves a process of mutual affirmation and admonition with regard to inherited confessional positions on scripture.[335] In the same way that there is no iner-

---

333. Wright, *The New Testament*, 32.
334. Heitink, *Practical Theology*, 196.
335. Fackre, *Restoring the Center*, 124.

rant biblical foundation, neither is there no inerrant biblical interpretation. Now, our approach to Scripture is one that attempts to listen to all interpretations of the biblical text—liberal and conservative, Catholic and Protestant, emerging church and African indigenous. The various insights and interpretations that each bring are held together in a web of belief, or a web of interpretation. I believe this is consistent with a chastened rationality and postfoundationalist approach. This web of interpretation must also heed the marginalized voices and interpretations of Scripture. This would allow it to take seriously the postmodern criticism of how knowledge and power are interrelated. Of course, such an approach requires the humility, of which we first spoke. The implications for practical theology then become clear. Practical theology, in its engagement with Scripture on any given issue (pastoral concern), should avail itself of the plurality of interpretations that are available. Are practical theologians ready for this challenge? Hastings believes that an ecumenical approach to practical theology has vast implications, including epistemological, for the discipline as a whole and not simply in ones approach to Scripture.[336] His approach though still has insights for our understanding of the ecumenical nature of Scripture. Whose interpretations do we engage with? Are we as practical theologians ecumenically involved worldwide or have we become captive to the turn to the local? Hastings notes that "In spite of the positive direction at the international discussion among practical theologians today, it must be admitted that this discussion has not yet discovered ways to fully include our colleagues in the non-western world."[337] Dreyer has noted that this remains a challenge for South African practical theologians, who find themselves more engaged with the non-Western world than perhaps their North American and European counterparts.[338] He argues that we need to become "more ecumenical in our research endeavours and to include denominations and religious traditions that are often marginalised in our research." An ecumenical approach to Scripture, while engaging meaningfully with our non-Western colleagues, would be one of the ways we could begin to engage with ecumenical issues within practical theology.

---

336. Hastings, *Practical Theology*, 29.
337. Ibid., 144.
338. Dreyer, "Practical Theology in SA," 7.

Coherency

Grenz[339] believes that Wolfhart Pannenberg is one theologian who has sought to move beyond foundationalism in his theological approach. Pannenberg feels a postfoundationalist perspective is one that best represents his approach.[340]

Important for Pannenberg, is whether theological truth coheres with other forms of knowledge. Coherence is not a new thing within theological circles as is evidenced by its use in the scholastic tradition. However, Pannenberg rejects the scholastics' attempt to reduce reason to simply illuminating truth that is presupposed to exist in revelation handed down through inspired Scripture.[341] Grenz notes that for Pannenberg, the danger here lies in

> [P]lacing the Bible in contradiction to every new discovery of truth, rather than integrating scientific discoveries into the truth claim of the Christian faith. In short, their doctrine of biblical inspiration failed to facilitate theologians in demonstrating the coherence of Christian doctrine with human knowledge.[342]

Pannenberg believes that truth must have a universal content, and further that it is displayed in history.[343] But, just in case we think Pannenberg argues for a rationalist certainty, he reminds us that all truth will be unveiled only at the end of history, at the eschaton. This means that our knowledge and belief remain partial at best. I believe that this approach is consistent with a critical realist approach. Grenz agrees while commenting on Pannenberg that he "draws from a coherentist approach in his attempt to carve out a theological method that is nonfoundational, yet committed to a realist metaphysic."[344]

The principle of coherence then becomes vital for any approach to understanding Scripture in critical realist sense. A postfoundational approach to Scripture asks itself whether the insights of Scripture, with reference to a given pastoral concern, cohere with other forms of knowledge. The very nature of the correlational hermeneutic aids this principle of coherence. As

---

339. Grenz, *Reason for Hope*, 15.
340. Schults, *Postfoundationalist Task*, ix.
341. Grenz, *Renewing the Center*, 196.
342. Ibid.
343. Ibid., 197.
344. Ibid.

one allows the knowledge base from the human sciences to be in dialogue with Scripture, one can begin to ask whether the insights of the human sciences cohere with the perspective of Scripture. Of course, this does not mean that if the human sciences disagree with Scripture, that the human sciences are automatically right. What it does, however, is give us pause for thought and further reflection and, if need be, revision.

Critical Realism

In our treatment of foundationalism and postfoundationalism, we have already discussed the importance of critical realism as a way of moving beyond foundationalism. We mentioned that when we examined the sources for practical theology, and specifically when addressing Scripture, it would again prove important. If this seems a strange thing to do, we have van Huyssteen to remind us that: "Personally I am convinced that no theologian who is trying to determine what the authority of the bible might mean today, and to identify the epistemological status of the bible in theological reflection, can avoid the important issues raised by some qualified forms of critical realism for theology."[345] One of the world's leading New Testament scholars admits that we can no longer simply approach the Bible in a modernistic enlightenment fashion. He also believes that critical realism is the best way forward.[346] With regard to the biblical text, critical realism steers a position between literalism and fictionalism.[347] Wright articulates it thus: "One meets it among naive theologians, who complain that while other people have 'pressupositions,' they simply read the text straight, or who claim that, because one cannot have 'direct access' to the 'facts' about Jesus, all that we are left with is a morass of first century fantasy."[348] Van Huyssteen speaks about how the Bible provides all the models that we might use for understanding our faith.[349] They might not be literal pictures, but are more than useful fictions. However, the Bible is crucial for affirming what we believe about God and his world:

---

345. van Huyssteen, *Essays in Postfoundationalist Theology*, 129.
346. Wright, *The New Testament*, 32.
347. van Huyssteen, *Essays in Postfoundationalist Theology*, 134.
348. Wright, *The New Testament*, 33.
349. van Huyssteen, *Essays in Postfoundationalist Theology*, 135.

> This text, as original witness to the events and person of our faith, in a very specific sense, is all we have. The metaphorical reference of its central concepts remains our only epistemic access to the God we believe in. Because of the importance of this fact, we can talk on an epistemological level about the realism of the text.[350]

An approach to the Bible that affirms the reality to which it speaks is important. This does not mean that it is infallible. Van Huyssteen quotes Peacocke in reminding us that our theologies can never be infallible, but some of them can be surer.[351] A critical realist understanding of the Scripture will help us with this. Scripture that is read humbly, ecumenically, and in a way that seeks to cohere with other knowledge forms will help us with the *critical* side of things. Wright reminds us that a critical realist approach to Scripture "leads to critical reflection on the products of our enquiry into 'reality', so that our assertions about 'reality' acknowledge their own provisionality. Knowledge, in other words, although in principle concerning realities independent of the knower, is never itself independent of the knower."[352] Perhaps Ganzevoort is right in arguing for the reliability of scripture as the best way for understanding it.[353]

Tradition

Scripture and tradition are often pitted against one other. When we think of Scripture, we think Protestantism. When we think of tradition, we think Catholicism. Often, in Protestantism, and specifically within evangelicalism, we find a very terse dismissal of tradition. Luther and his call for *sola scriptura* is evangelicalism's mantra. What follows will attempt to describe the importance of tradition as representing a vital resource for practical theology, and will argue that, in fact, a fresh engagement with the different church traditions is a healthy route in moving beyond foundationalism.

When, in theological reflection, we dealt with the role of Scripture, we noted in some detail questions regarding inerrancy. We rejected inerrancy in our use of Scripture for various reasons, and noted its epistemological affinity with foundationalism. Yet, for sectors of the Christian community, the infallibility of tradition has also been a hotly contested issue. Hans Küng's

---

350. Ibid., 49.
351. Ibid., 161.
352. Wright, *The New Testament*, 35.
353. Ganzevoort, "The Splintered Cross," 56.

lifelong battle with the magisterium within the Roman Catholic Church is well known.[354] In his short little book, *Infallible?*, he seeks to bring to light some of the faults and dangers of infallibility for tradition, as represented by the magisterium. He states his view tersely: "The errors of the Church's teaching office have been numerous and grave; nowadays, when an open discussion can no longer be forbidden, they cannot be denied even by the more conservative theologians and church leaders."[355] He then proceeds to give a long list of the various errors that the Pope and the magisterium have committed, and where the church's tradition has in fact proved to be false.

The Roman Catholic Church is more forthright in admitting the infallibility of the church's tradition, as interpreted and given voice in the magisterium. Evangelicals claim differently, but also are not immune to the charge of making their tradition infallible. McGrath notes that what often happens is an affirmation of the inerrancy of the evangelical tradition represented by the various Reformational confessions.[356]

Without going into great detail, this can be witnessed in the debate regarding justification by faith, to which McGrath alluded. The fact that justification is concerned with how the gentiles are to be included as part of God's family and has very little to do with individual salvation, is now generally accepted by most Pauline scholars.[357] Luther's understanding of justification by faith is concerned more with medieval Catholicism than with what Paul actually said.[358] That some within evangelicalism cannot accept this is perhaps due to the fact that they might give their confessional tradition too high a standing. This is demonstrated specifically in the work of John Piper's response to N. T. Wright's understanding of justification.

Despite all the debates around the inerrancy of tradition, whether overt or subtle, it still remains a vital tool for theological reflection, as McGrath notes:

> One of the greatest tragedies that has beset Protestant churches in the present century is a loss of corporate, long term memory, in favour of a time-scale that spans at best a generation. When you're trying to get somewhere, it helps to know where you've come from. Hindsight leads to foresight, as an enhanced awareness of

---

354. Küng, *Infallible?*, 27.
355. Ibid.
356. McGrath, "Evangelical Theological Method," 31.
357. Harink, *Paul among the Postliberals*, 29.
358. Wright, *What St. Paul Really Said*, 114.

Postfoundationalist Reflections in Practical Theology

possibilities dawns. There is a need to recover and value the hard won insights of earlier generations, and incorporate them into our thinking.[359]

Negatively, a postfoundationalist perspective with regard to tradition would have to resist anyone who claims to accurately represent either the Bible, God, or any other inerrant position. Positively, a postfoundationalist approach toward tradition would affirm that tradition, represented by the Christian tradition, has been a vehicle for God to speak to the world through his Spirit. Tradition seeks to embody, as best it can, the faith communities' understanding of God, and indeed even its participation with God in mission. There was a form of tradition that was located within the early Christian communities before Scripture was written. In fact, even after Scripture was written, it was the living tradition of the church that authorized which texts were deemed to be authoritative.[360] The biblical texts were regarded as the vehicle through which the Spirit addressed the community. It was the illuminating work of the Spirit that brought forth the Scriptures from the community, and that illumination does not cease with the closing of the canon.[361] Therefore, the Spirit enables the church to apply the Scriptures afresh in its own context.

To understand the role of the Spirit is essential in understanding a postfoundationalist approach to tradition. Grenz and Franke explain:

> A nonfoundational understanding of Scripture and tradition locates ultimate authority only in the action of the triune God. If we must speak of a "foundation" of the Christian faith at all, then, we must speak of neither Scripture nor tradition in and of themselves, but only of the triune God who is disclosed in polyphonic fashion through Scripture, the church, and even the world.[362]

As with Scripture, an ecumenical approach to tradition is another way to guard against a foundationalist approach to tradition. By listening to a variety of voices in an ecumenical spirit, we are able to guard against the abuse of knowledge and the insularity of one's own tradition. In the same way that we argued that a postfoundationalist approach to Scripture ought to be humble, so it is with tradition. In this way, we allow for

---

359. McGrath, *Roots That Refresh*, 21.
360. Grenz and Franke, *Beyond Foundationalism*, 115.
361. Ibid., 116.
362. Ibid., 117.

A Postfoundationalist Practical Theology

the opportunity for mutual correction.[363] We are far more likely to gain a correct understanding of what the Spirit might be saying through the churches, by listening to the multiple traditions within the churches. What is being affirmed here is a *community of communities* that are all legitimate expressions and understandings of the one true church.[364]

A postfoundational appropriation of the churches' tradition within a correlational hermeneutic must therefore reject a totalizing of one's own tradition, whether in confessional statements, or embodied in practice. Despite this, the Spirit still speaks through the church's tradition. In order to discern the voice of the Spirit through tradition, one needs to maintain a humble and ecumenical position, consummate with a postfoundationalist epistemology.

The Mediation of Scripture and Tradition for Practical Theology

This is another point where practical theology walks on the boundaries, and is open to criticism as being far too eclectic. For, in order for practical theologians to engage with the Christian classics as part of a correlational hermeneutic, they must heed other theological traditions. This is even more difficult, as each tradition has its own hermeneutical positions and self-regulating conversations. But, this cannot be avoided. Hendriks lists how these disciplines are used in mediating the Christian classics of Scripture and tradition:

> The biblical disciplines of Old and New Testament Studies specialize in understanding the biblical text; Systematic Theology or Dogmatics have organized the content of Scripture in various ways using different methods; philosophical and comparative religious studies play a role; ethical debates have taken place; and church history tells the ongoing story of the church in the world.[365]

To my mind, practical theology, without the aid of these disciplines, would remain seriously handicapped. We have noted Graham et al., and their comments with regard to Scripture and practical theology.[366] They further argue that theological reflection has been extremely weak in its use

---

363. Fackre, *Restoring the Center*, 118.
364. Webber, *Ancient-Future Faith*, 85.
365. Hendriks, *Studying Congregations in Africa*, 29.
366. Graham et al., *Theological Reflection*, 7.

of the traditional theological disciplines. They further note that practical theologians are far more equipped in dealing with understanding local contexts and socio-economic realities than engaging with church history, doctrine, and the Bible. They believe that the main cause is the separation of theological reflection from systematics, historical theology and the biblical disciplines in theological courses and curricula.[367] Ward also argues for practical theology to engage with the other theological disciplines.[368] He also laments the fact that practical theology is so fearful of doctrine, or specifically theological statements.

It is my contention that the rush to the practical in practical theology, as already noted, is partly to blame for the scepticism or even disdain toward the traditional disciplines. I believe that, in future, a far closer relationship between practical theology and the other theological disciplines must be worked out. It is also incumbent upon academic practical theologians to try to keep abreast of various developments within the other disciplines. As it was with the human sciences, a use of the other theological disciplines will most likely result in the use of secondary sources. It is also important to have access to archives and resources in the other disciplines, which can be utilized with reference to the various pastoral concerns that are to be reflected upon.

A Postfoundational Critical Correlational Hermeneutic

In this section, an attempt was made to show how the two sources of a correlational hermeneutic engage with the human sciences and the Christian classics. It argued for a specific understanding of this correlation that remains open to mutual correction and affirmation (hence critical). It was argued that when engaging with both sources, a postfoundationalist approach must be taken. This move beyond foundationalism has been due to the postmodern shift and the hermeneutical turn. A postfoundationalist approach to epistemology leads to a rejection of understanding truth in an absolute sense, and is characterized by a chastened rationality seen in the position of critical realism. Taking these epistemological concerns into account, both sources engage with each other and with the given pastoral concern (that has arisen out of experience in a local context). At this point,

---

367. Ibid.
368. Ward, "The Hermeneutical," 58, 60.

we move to the last section for our discussion, and conclude our hermeneutical circle—action.

PASTORAL RESPONSE

In this brief closing section, we bring our pastoral cycle to full circle. Moving from practice (the local experiential reality) to theory (correlational hermeneutic), we now return to practice. This pastoral cycle leads to real action and change in a real world. It is not good enough for theoretical proposals to remain theoretical. Here practical theology is affirmed as *inherently transformative* and seeks to transform life.[369] As already noted, the limited nature of knowledge and our ability to understand reality, which a postfoundational approach requires, leads to an affirmation of the pastoral cycle, for the pastoral cycle has no end as it returns to practice in the pastoral response, which then becomes a source of theological reflection. It is here that the hope that a form of practical life wisdom emerges from one's "theological endeavour"[370] which leads to a transforming or transformative practice.[371]

A pastoral response, and a missional praxis-based theology, moves out into the life and witness of the church and brings about aspects of God's eschatological future.[372] It is important for practical theology not just to rest when the theoretical work has been done, and when it has proposals for action. It must actually intervene in that pastoral concern.[373] Miller-McLemore in a penetrating article entitled "The 'Clerical' Paradigm: a Fallacy of Misplaced Concreteness" highlights the fact that practical theology has been particularly bad at this juncture.

> In descriptions of practical theology, interpretation has been key. Action and implementation are often afterthoughts, even though both of these are understood as important elements in the science of hermeneutics. Practical theologian Don Browning, paraphrasing Richard Bernstein and Hans-Georg Gadamer, says that in the practical wisdom necessary for ministry, "understanding, interpretation, *and application* are not distinct but intimately related."

369. Maddox, "The Recovery," 667.
370. Nell, "Practical Theology," 8.
371. Couture, *Blessed Are the Poor?*, 25.
372. Hendriks, *Studying Congregations in Africa*, 33.
373. De Kock, "Open Seminary at Tabor," 8.

> Major spokespersons in practical theology such as Browning and Farley, however, have had immense interest in the first two: understanding and interpretation. They have had less to say about "application."[374]

It is important to remember the groundwork that was laid earlier in our discussion of practical theology's missional nature and theological reflection. It was argued that all of life is under the scope of God's mission and that he is missional by nature. The implication drawn was that all of life can come under the *scope* of practical theology. Any part of life can become the raw material of pastoral concern, as it arises out of local realities and real lived experience. As it was with our starting point, so it must be with our ending point. Hendriks argues that action should be expressed at five levels: personal, ecclesiastical, secular, scientific, and ecological.[375] These five dimensions are regarded as helpful in capturing the scope and breadth of theological reflection. However, I think that reflection on a pastoral concern must not speak to all of these areas simultaneously. The given area from which a pastoral concern arises would also be the area where an intervention will be done. Of course, this does not mean that there will not be any implications for the other areas, but it does imply that it might not.

The importance of action, as the conclusion of the pastoral cycle, must not lead to a now static conclusion of the theological process. The important and neglected question[376] for practical theology as to what we can hope for, and how we do that, now rises to the fore. The process is circular, and intervention must lead to further reflection. We are never really finished as Veling notes: "practical theology wants to keep our relationship with the world open, so that we are never quite 'done' with things; rather, always undoing and redoing them, so that we can keep the 'doing' happening, passionate, keen, expectant—never satisfied, never quite finished."[377] Hence, the proposals for action, and the action itself, will take on a largely provisional nature. It is also provisional in the sense that all action will ultimately find its fulfilment and perfection at the eschaton. When God comes to restore the earth and cosmos in all its dimensions, there will be a completion of all our good works. We act also because we believe that God

---

374. Miller-McLemore, "The "Clerical Paradigm," 28.
375. Hendriks, *Studying Congregations in Africa*, 33.
376. Louw, "Creative Hope and Imagination," 336.
377. Veling, *Practical Theology*, 7.

will not obliterate all our good deeds and the earth that we now inhabit. God is in the business of restoration, not simply destruction.

Our intervention in people's real lives and the planet ought also to be conducted with a great deal of humility and sensitivity. Humility that knowledge can very easily be used to exploit and control, rather than liberate. Humble, also in the sense that it is God who is already acting, and it is the Triune God whose mission we are now joining.

We are also sensitive to people's real needs; we do not intervene in a colonial manner. By this is meant that we do not act out of a sense of our superiority and belief in the rightness of our knowledge; we act in partnership with, and for, the other.

At this point, the various ethical considerations as to how one brings about change and how one conducts oneself while acting, will be avoided. Certainly, at the secular or public level there could be a call for action that might result in certain actions that could result in the law being broken. Equally so, reflection on the role of women in ministry in an ecclesial setting might require one to take a stand that might result in one's excommunication. These are difficult issues, which need to be evaluated in their own right. At this point, what is being argued for is simply that one must act once the theoretical reflection has taken place. One must act because practical theology is missional and, to be engaged in mission, is to act.

FIVE

Conclusion

From the beginning, an attempt was sought to define what a practical theological approach that has moved beyond foundationalism would look like. This was done by examining foundationalism's historical development from Descartes through to Kant, and an argument was presented that foundationalism was one of the central tenets of modernism, as expressed in the Enlightenment. Both rationalism and empiricism were influenced by this foundationalist paradigm.

Then the postmodern critique of modernistic assumptions about knowledge and reality and how the modern project collapsed was examined. A detailed discussion of the growth of postfoundationalism, which takes seriously the postmodern critique, was then explored. Then, it was proposed that a form of critical realism is a good option for moving beyond foundationalism.

The section that followed attempted to examine the discipline of practical theology in detail, in order to discover whether it had indeed moved beyond the modern foundationalist paradigm. However, before doing this, we sought to lay a definitional, methodological, and historical foundation with regard to practical theology. Definitionally, three separate terms—pastoral theology, practical theology and theological reflection—were examined. Practical theology was chosen, as referring to the more formal and academic dimensions, while theological reflection was used in a broader sense. It was noted that there are similarities between practical theology and theological reflection, but also important distinctions—the obvious being that anyone would be capable of doing some form of theological reflection.

Postfoundationalist Reflections in Practical Theology

Moving on from there, we sought to examine the historical development of practical theology as a discipline. This was to demonstrate the move from an applied theological methodology to a more praxis-based methodology consistent with a move beyond foundationalism.

This historical development involved examining practical theology within the broader theological conversation with regard to how theology had become fragmented. Leaning heavily on the work of Farley, we tried to show how the discipline fragmented while, at the same time, pointing out the rise of practical theology as a sub-discipline within theology as a whole. Then it was noted that certain developments in the latter half of the twentieth century led to a rethinking with regard to the nature of practical theology. Developments within practical philosophy, as well as influences from liberation theology, brought this on. I concluded that practical theology is no longer viewed as an applied theology, but rather one whose domain involves the very practical and earthly dimensions of our existence. It was demonstrated how practical theology had indeed made moves beyond foundationalism. Snapshots of certain developments in different regions of the world were given in an attempt to illustrate this.

After laying the above foundations, an attempt was made to flesh out in greater detail what a postfoundationalist approach would look like following on from the above developments. The missional discussion of practical theology was entered into by first examining the question of mission. The problem of missions and how they have been perceived was noted. An attempt was also made to place the missional question within an historical context. This was done with the help of David Bosch's *Transforming Mission*. Bosch illustrates the various paradigms within mission—firstly in the Bible and then how it has been understood in church history. Flowing from this discussion, it was demonstrated how incorrect understandings of the church and her relationship to the kingdom can lead to a defunct theology. It was also mentioned that one's understanding of personal salvation and cosmic redemption shapes one's views. This discussion led to a conclusion that mission is broader than the church, yet the church remains central. A further conclusion was that mission cannot be seen in a personal salvific sense only, but involves the whole of God's created order.

Then, we engaged with a Trinitarian understanding of mission and argued for the importance of understanding the missionary nature of the Triune God. This was done with the help of Newbigin and his views regarding the Father, the Son, and Spirit within mission. Leading on from understanding God as missional, it was argued that the church is also to be regarded as missional in its nature and purpose. The conclusions drawn from the engagement with the missional question (understood in a trinitarian sense and with reference to the church) led to the conclusion that practical theology is also a missional discipline. As God and the church's mission is broad and involves all of life, so too are practical theology and its theological reflection broad and involve all of life. Practical theology is at the service of God and the church in reflection upon, and participation in, God's mission in the world in all its varying dimensions. This could also be called a *holistic practical theology*. The above missional framework provided a lens to examine the pastoral cycle, a correlational hermeneutic, and contextual approach consistent with a postfoundationalist approach.

It was mentioned that the pastoral cycle is the most helpful way to understand the theological reflective process, and one that is consistent with the provisional nature of our knowledge and postfoundationalism. The first stage of the pastoral cycle, as a starting point for reflection, was to look at the local situation and one's experience of that situation. In understanding this local experiential reality, one needs to take both local and global factors into account—hence a glocal approach to practical theology.

This pastoral concern is included in the second part of the pastoral cycle, which is of a more theoretical nature. Here, it was argued for a specific understanding of the correlational hermeneutic that takes into account both the human sciences and the Christian classics. It was demonstrated that, in dealing with both the sciences and the Christian classics one must take into account epistemological shifts and the decline of the Enlightenment paradigm. Therefore, the argument was for a postfoundationalist approach to both sides of the correlational hermeneutic. Once the raw material from the glocal experience of the pastoral concern is taken into dialogue correlationally with the human sciences and the Christian classics, a proposal for action must be decided upon. However, in order to complete the pastoral cycle, it must actually lead to action and some form of intervention. This ought to be done in a responsible and sensitive manner. This practice to theory and back to practice again, the researcher believes is a praxis-based approach to practical theology, consistent with a move beyond foundationalism.

Indeed, practical theology has come a long way from the confines of the foundationalist modern paradigm. Its emphasis on the local, its critical correlational approach and emphasis on the pastoral cycle are a few examples of how the postmodern critique has been taken seriously, and a truly postfoundationalist approach to practical theology has emerged, and is emerging. Further reflection on how postfoundationalism can aid, and give sharper focus to aspects of practical theology, must continue. It is hoped that this book has contributed to this in some small way.

Bibliography

Anderson, Dick. *We Felt like Grasshoppers: The Story of Africa Inland Mission*. Wheaton: Crossway, 1994.
Anderson, Ray Sherman. *The Shape of Practical Theology: Empowering Ministry with Theological Praxis*. Downers Grove, IL: InterVarsity, 2001.
Armstrong, Karen. *Islam: A Short History*. London: Phoenix, 2002.
Astley, Jeff. *Ordinary Theology: Looking, Listening, and Learning in Theology*. Hampshire: Ashgate, 2002.
Augsburger, D. W. *Pastoral Counseling across Cultures*. Philadelphia: Westminster John Knox, 1986.
Babbie, Earl R. *The Practice of Social Research*. 10th ed. Belmont, CA: Wadsworth, 2004.
Ballard, Paul H. "The Emergence of Pastoral and Practical Theology in Britain." In *The Blackwell Reader in Pastoral and Practical Theology*, edited by J. Woodward and S. Pattison, 59–72. Oxford, UK: Blackwell, 2000.
———. "The Use of Scripture." In *The Wiley-Blackwell Companion to Practical Theology*, edited by B. Miller-McLemore, 163–72. West Sussex: Blackwell, 2012.
Ballard, Paul H., and John Pritchard. *Practical Theology in Action: Christian Thinking in the Service of Church and Society*. London: SPCK, 2006.
Baronov, David. *The Conceptual Foundations of Social Research Methods*. Boulder, CO: Paradigm, 2004.
Barth, Karl. *Dogmatics in Outline*. London: SCM, 1966.
Basney, Lionel. *An Earth-Careful Way of Life: Christian Stewardship and the Environmental Crisis*. Downers Grove, IL: InterVarsity, 1994.
Bass, D. C. "Introduction." In *Practicing Theology: Beliefs and Practices in Christian Life*, edited by Miroslav Volf and Dorthy C. Bass, 1–9. Grand Rapids: Eerdmans, 2002.
Bass, Dorothy C., and Craig R. Dykstra. *For Life Abundant: Practical Theology, Theological Education, and Christian Ministry*. Grand Rapids: Eerdmans, 2008.
Bell, Rob. *Love Wins: A Book about Heaven, Hell, and the Fate of Every Person Who Ever Lived*. New York: HarperOne, 2011.
Bennett, Zoe. "Britain." In *The Wiley-Blackwell Companion to Practical Theology*, edited by Bonnie J. Miller-McLemore. Sussex: Blackwell, 2012.
Bennett, Zoe, and Elaine Louise Graham. "The Professional Doctorate in Practical Theology: Developing the Researching Professional in Practical Theology in Higher Education." *Journal of Adult Theological Education* 5:1 (2008) 33–51.
Benson, B. "Theology and (Non)(Post) Foundationalism." In *A New Kind of Conversation: Blogging Toward a Postmodern Faith*. Colorado Springs, CO: Paternoster, 2007.
Berkhof, Louis. *Systematic Theology*. Edinburgh: Banner of Truth, 1939.

Bibliography

Bevans, Stephen B. *Models of Contextual Theology.* Maryknoll, NY: Orbis, 2002.

Bhaskar, Roy. *A Realist Theory of Science.* Abingdon: Routledge, 2008.

Bhaskar, Roy, and Mervyn Hartwig. *The Formation of Critical Realism: A Personal Perspective.* Abingdon: Routledge, 2010.

Boff, Clodovis. *Theology and Praxis: Epistemological Foundations.* Maryknoll, NY: Orbis, 1987.

Bonino, Jose Míguez. *Revolutionary Theology Comes of Age.* London: SPCK, 1975.

Borg, Marcus J. *The God We Never Knew: Beyond Dogmatic Religion to a More Authentic Contemporary Faith.* San Francisco: HarperSanFrancisco, 1997.

Bosch, David Jacobus. *Transforming Mission: Paradigm Shifts in Theology of Mission.* Maryknoll, NY: Orbis, 1991.

Browning, Don S. *A Fundamental Practical Theology: Descriptive and Strategic Proposals.* Minneapolis: Fortress, 1991.

Büchner, Elsje P., and Julian C. Müller. "The Story of the Department of Practical Theology." *Verbum Et Ecclesia* 30:3 (1970) 153.

Burger, Coenie. *Praktiese Teologie in Suid-Afrika: 'n Ondersoek Na Die Denke Oor Sekere Voorvrae Van Die Vak.* Pretoria, South Africa: RGN, 1991.

Cahalan, Kathleen. "Locating Practical Theology in Catholic Theological Discourse and Practice." *International Journal of Practical Theology* 15:1 (2011) 1–21.

Cahalan, Kathleen, and J. R. Nieman. "Mapping the Field of Practical Theology." In *For Life Abundant: Practical Theology, Theological Education, and Christian Ministry,* edited by Dorothy C. Bass and Craig Dykstra, 62–90. Grand Rapids: Eerdmans, 2008.

Cahalan, Kathleen et al. "Teaching Practical Theology: Introducing Six Perspectives." *International Journal of Practical Theology* 12:1 (2008) 35–87.

Cameron, Helen et al. *Talking about God in Practice: Theological Action Research and Practical Theology.* London: SCM, 2010.

Capps, D. *Living Stories: Pastoral Counseling in Congregational Context.* Minneapolis: Fortress, 1988.

Carson, D. A. *Becoming Conversant with the Emerging Church: Understanding a Movement and Its Implications.* Grand Rapids: Zondervan, 2005.

Cartledge, Mark J. "Affective Theological Practice." *International Journal of Practical Theology* 8:1 (2004) 34–52.

Castells, Manuel. *End of Millennium.* Oxford: Blackwell, 2000.

———. *The Information Age: Economy, Society and Culture.* Vol. 2. Malden, MA: Blackwell, 2004.

Chopp, R. B. "Educational Process, Feminist Practice." *Christian Century* 112:4 (1995) 111–16.

Chung, Hyun Kyung. *Struggle to Be the Sun Again: Introducing Asian Women's Theology.* London: SCM, 1990.

Cochrane, James R., John De Gruchy, and Robin Petersen. *In Word and in Deed: Towards a Practical Theology of Social Transformation: A Framework for Reflection and Training.* Pietermaritzburg, South Africa: Cluster, 1991.

Collier, Andrew. *Critical Realism: An Introduction to Roy Bhaskar's Philosophy.* London: Verso, 1994.

Cone, James H. *Teologia Nera Della Liberazione E Black Power [A Black Theology of Liberation].* Maryknoll, NY: Orbis, 1990.

Couture, Pamela D. *Blessed Are the Poor?: Women's Poverty, Family Policy, and Practical Theology.* Nashville: Abingdon, 1991.

Cronshaw, Darren. "Reenvisioning Theological Education, Mission and the Local Church." *Mission Studies* 28:1 (2011) 91–115.

Crossan, John Dominic. "The Resurrection: Historical Event or Theological Explanation." In *The Resurrection of Jesus: John Dominic Crossan and N.T. Wright in Dialogue*, edited by Robert B. Stewart, 16–47. Minneapolis: Fortress, 2006.

De Gruchy, J. *Being Human: Confessions of a Christian Humanist.* London: SCM, 2006.

———. "The Nature, Necessity and Task of Theology." In *Doing Theology in Context: South African Perspectives.* Maryknoll, NY: Orbis, 1994.

De Kock, Wynand. "Open Seminary at Tabor. Master of Arts in Church Practice." No pages. Online: www.tabor.vic.edu.au/files/publications/course-promo/2009-MACP-information-booklet.pdf.

———. "Open Seminary." Openseminary.com. No pages. Online: www.openseminary.com.

Dingemans, Gijsbert D. J. "Practical Theology in the Academy: A Contemporary Overview." *The Journal of Religion* 76:1 (1996) 82–96.

Donovan, Vincent J. *Christianity Rediscovered: An Epistle from the Masai.* Maryknoll, NY: SCM, 1978.

Dreyer, J. "Practical Theology in SA: Recent Developments and New Challenges." Unpublished Paper Presented at SPTSA, University of South Africa, 2010.

Dulles, A. "Pannenberg on Revelation and Faith." In *The Theology of Wolfart Pannenberg*, edited by Braaten and Clayton, 169–87. Minneapolis: Augsburg, 1988.

Erickson, Millard J. *Christian Theology.* Bassingstoke, UK: Marshall Pickering, 1983.

———. *The Evangelical Left: Encountering Postconservative Evangelical Theology.* Grand Rapids: Baker, 1997.

Fackre, Gabriel. *Restoring the Center: Essays Evangelical and Ecumenical.* Downers Grove, IL: InterVarsity, 1998.

Farley, Edward. *Theologia: The Fragmentation and Unity of Theological Education.* Philadelphia: Fortress, 1994.

Farley, R. "Interpreting Situations: An Enquiry into the Nature of Practical Theology." In *The Blackwell Reader in Pastoral and Practical Theology*, edited by James Woodward and Stephen Pattison, 118–27. Oxford: Blackwell, 2000.

Firet, Jacob. *Dynamics in Pastoring.* Grand Rapids: Eerdmans, 1986.

Fleetwood, Steve, editor. *Critical Realism in Economics: Development and Debate.* New York: Routledge, 1999.

Fowler, J. W. "Practical Theology and the Shaping of Christian Lives." In *Practical Theology: The Emerging Field in Theology, Church and World*, edited by D. S. Browning, 148–66. San Francisco: Harper & Row, 1983.

———. *Stages of Faith: The Psychology of Human Development and the Quest for Meaning.* San Francisco: Harper & Row, 1981.

Franke, John R. *The Character of Theology: An Introduction to Its Nature, Task, and Purpose.* Grand Rapids: Baker Academic, 2005.

Frost, Michael, and Alan Hirsch. *The Shaping of Things to Come: Innovation and Mission for the 21st-Century Church.* Peabody, MA: Hendrickson, 2003.

Ganzevoort, R. R. "Forks in the Road When Tracing the Sacred. Practical Theology as Hermeneutics of Lived Religion." Presidential address, International Academy of Practical Theology, Chicago, August 3, 2009.

———. "The Social Construction of Revelation." *International Journal of Practical Theology* 8:2 (2006) 1–14.

Bibliography

———. "The Splintered Cross." In *Met Het Oog Op Morgen: Ecclesiologische Beschouwingen Aangeboden Aan Jan Visser*, edited by Hallebeek and Wirix, 46–57. Zoetermeer, The Netherlands: Boekencentrum, 1996.

———. "Strange Bedfellows or Siamese Twins? The Search for the Sacred in Practical Theology and Psychology of Religion." Proceedings of The Relation between Psychology of Religion and Practical Theology, Amsterdam, 2010.

———. "Teaching Religion in a Plural World." Edited by N. Lantinga, 117–24. Proceedings of International Conference of IAPCHE, Granada, Nicaragua. Sioux Center Iowa: Dordt College Press, 2008.

Giles, K. "The Subordination of Christ and the Subordination of Women." In *Discovering Biblical Equality: Complementarity without Hierarchy*, edited by Ronald W. Pierce, Rebecca M. Groothuis, and Gordon D. Fee, 334–52. Downers Grove, IL: InterVarsity, 2004.

Goheen, Michael W. *"As the Father Has Sent Me, I Am Sending You": J.E. Lesslie Newbigin's Missionary Ecclesiology*. Zoetermeer, The Netherlands: Boekencentrum, 2000.

Graham, Elaine L. et al. *Theological Reflection: Methods*. London: SCM, 2005.

Gräb, Wilhelm. "Practical Theology as Theology of Religion. Schleiermacher's Understanding of Practical Theology as a Discipline." *International Journal of Practical Theology* 9:2 (2005) 181–96.

Grenz, Stanley J. *The Millennial Maze: Sorting out Evangelical Options*. Downers Grove, IL: InterVarsity, 1992.

———. *A Primer on Postmodernism*. Grand Rapids: Eerdmans, 1996.

———. *Renewing the Center: Evangelical Theology in a Post-Theological Era*. Grand Rapids: Baker Academic, 2000.

———. *The Moral Quest: Foundations of Christian Ethics*. Downers Grove, IL: InterVarsity, 1997.

———. *Reason for Hope: The Systematic Theology of Wolfhart Pannenberg*. Grand Rapids: Eerdmans, 2005.

———. *Rediscovering the Triune God: The Trinity in Contemporary Theology*. Minneapolis: Fortress, 2004.

———. *Revisioning Evangelical Theology: A Fresh Agenda for the 21st Century*. Downers Grove, IL: InterVarsity, 1993.

———. *Theology for the Community of God*. Grand Rapids: Eerdmans, 1994.

Grenz, Stanley J., and John R. Franke. *Beyond Foundationalism: Shaping Theology in a Postmodern Context*. Louisville: Westminster John Knox, 2001.

Grenz, Stanley J., and Roger E. Olson. *Twentieth Century Theology: God and the World in a Transitional Age*. Downers Grove, IL: InterVarsity, 1992.

———. *Who Needs Theology?: An Invitation to the Study of God*. Downers Grove: InterVarsity, 1996.

Grudem, Wayne A. *Systematic Theology: An Introduction to Biblical Doctrine*. Leicester, UK: Inter-Varsity, 1994.

Guder, Darrell L. *The Continuing Conversion of the Church*. Grand Rapids: Eerdmans, 2000.

Hanson, Paul D. *The People Called: The Growth of Community in the Bible*. San Francisco: Harper & Row, 1986.

Harink, Doug. *Paul among the Postliberals: Pauline Theology beyond Christendom and Modernity*. Grand Rapids: Brazos, 2003.

Bibliography

Hastings, Thomas John. *Practical Theology and the One Body of Christ: Toward a Missional-ecumenical Model.* Grand Rapids: Eerdmans, 2007.

Hazle, Dave. "Practical Theology Today And The Implications For Mission." *International Review of Mission* 92:366 (2003) 345–55.

Heimbrock, Hans-Günter. "From Data to Theory: Elements of Methodology in Empirical Phenomenological Research in Practical Theology." *International Journal of Practical Theology* 9:2 (2005) 273–99.

———. "Practical Theology as Empirical Theology." *International Journal of Practical Theology* 14:2 (2011) 153–70.

Heitink, Gerben. *Practical Theology: History, Theory, Action Domains: Manual for Practical Theology.* Translated by Reinder Bruinsma. Grand Rapids: Eerdmans, 1999.

Hendriks, H. J. "Developing a Contextual, Missional Ecclesiology in a Congregation Using a Practical Theological Methodology." *Praktiese Teologie in SA* 16:1 (2001) 1–18.

———. *The Future of the Church, the Church of the Future.* Wellington, New Zealand: Hugenote, 1992.

———. "The Future of the Church, the Church of the Future." Lecture, Universiteit Stellenboach Drukkery, 2003.

———. *Studying Congregations in Africa.* Wellington, New Zealand: Lux Verbi, 2004.

Hiebert, Paul G. *Anthropological Reflections on Missiological Issues.* Grand Rapids: Baker, 1994.

Hurding, R. *Root and Shoots: A Guide to Counselling and Psychotherapy.* London: Hodder & Stoughton, 1986.

Johnson, Burke, and Larry B. Christensen. *Educational Research: Quantitative, Qualitative, and Mixed Approaches.* 4th ed. Los Angeles: Sage, 2012.

Johnson, Paul. *A History of the American People.* London: Phoenix, 1997.

Kelsey, David H. *To Understand God Truly: What's Theological about a Theological School.* Louisville: Westminster John Knox, 1992.

Kelty, Brian J. "Practical Theology in Australia." *International Journal of Practical Theology* 9:1 (2005) 140–55.

Kim, Hyun-Sook. "The Hermeneutical-Praxis Paradigm and Practical Theology." *Religious Education* 102:4 (2007) 419–36.

Koopman, Nico. "Some Contours for Public Theology in South Africa." *International Journal of Practical Theology* 14:1 (2010) 123–38.

Kretzschmar, L. "Ethics in a Theological Context." In *Theology and Praxis. Doing Ethics in Context: South African Perspectives*, edited by C. Villa-Vicencio and J. De Gruchy, 2–23. Maryknoll, NY: Orbis, 1994.

———. "Introduction: Studying at UNISA." Online lecture, Invitation to Theology: Fundamental Module for BTH Programmes CGM101-L, UNISA, 2000.

Küng, Hans. *Credo: The Apostle's Creed Explained for Today.* London: SCM, 1993.

———. *Does God Exist?* London: Collins, 1978.

———. *Infallible?* London: Collins, 1970.

Ladd, George Eldon. *A Theology of the New Testament.* Grand Rapids: Eerdmans, 1974.

Latourette, Kenneth Scott. *A History of the Expansion of Christianity: The First Five Centuries.* Vol. 1. London: Eyre & Spottiswoode, 1943.

Louw, Daniël. "Creative Hope and Imagination in a Practical Theology of Aesthetic (Artistic) Reason." *Religion and Theology* 8:3 (2001) 327–44.

———. *A Pastoral Hermeneutics of Care and Encounter: A Theological Design for a Basic Theory, Anthropology, Method, and Therapy.* Wellington, New Zealand: Lux Verbi, 1998.

Bibliography

Lynch, Gordon, and Stephen Pattison. "Exploring Positive Learning Experiences in the Context of Practical Theological Education." *Teaching Theology and Religion* 8:3 (2005) 144–54.

MacGavran, Donald A. *Understanding Church Growth.* Grand Rapids: Eerdmans, 1970.

Maddox, Randy L. "The Recovery of Theology as a Practical Discipline." *Theological Studies* 51:4 (1990) 650–72.

Mason, Jennifer. *Qualitative Researching.* London: Sage, 2002.

McGrath, Alister. "Evangelical Theological Method: The State of the Art." In *Evangelical Futures: A Conversation on Theological Method*, edited by J. G. Stackhouse, 15–38. Grand Rapids: Baker Academic, 2000.

———. *A Fine-Tuned Universe: The Quest for God in Science and Theology.* Louisville: Westminster John Knox, 2009.

———. *Roots That Refresh: A Celebration of Reformational Spirituality.* London: Hodder & Stoughton, 1991.

———. *A Scientific Theology.* Grand Rapids: Eerdmans, 2002.

McLaren, Brian D. "Church Emerging: Or Why I Still Use the Term *Postmodern* but with Mixed Feelings." In *An Emergent Manifesto of Hope*, edited by Doug Paggit and Tony Jones, 141–52. Grand Rapids: Baker, 2007.

———. *A Generous Orthodoxy.* Grand Rapids: Zondervan, 2004.

———. *The Last Word and the Word after That: A Tale of Faith, Doubt, and a New Kind of Christianity.* San Francisco: Jossey-Bass, 2005.

———. *A New Kind of Christian: A Tale of Two Friends on a Spiritual Journey.* San Francisco: Jossey-Bass, 2001.

———. *The Secret Message of Jesus: Uncovering the Truth That Could Change Everything.* Nashville: W Pub., 2006.

Miller-McLemore, Bonnie J. "The 'Clerical Paradigm': A Fallacy of Misplaced Concreteness?" *International Journal of Practical Theology* 11:1 (2007) 19–38.

———. *The Wiley-Blackwell Companion to Practical Theology.* Oxford: Blackwell, 2012.

Moltmann, Jürgen. *Theology of Hope: On the Ground and the Implications of a Christian Eschatology.* London: SCM, 1967.

Moore, Mary Elizabeth. "Editorial Practical Theology: Bound by a Common Center or Thin Threads?" *International Journal of Practical Theology* 10:2 (2007) 163–67.

Mouton, J. *How to Succeed in Your Master's and Doctoral Studies: A South African Guide and Resource Book.* Pretoria, South Africa: Van Schaik, 2001.

Mosmi, V. "Recent Trends in Practical Theology." *Bulletin for Contextual Theology* 1. No pages. Online: www.sorat.ukzn.ac.za/theology/bct/msomi.htm.

Müller, Julian. "HIV/AIDS, Narrative Practical Theology, and Postfoundationalism: The Emergence of a New Story." *HTS Teologiese Studies/Theological Studies* 60:1/2 (2004) 293–306.

———. "Holistic Pastoral Ministry in a Time of Transition." Proceedings of Joint Conference of Academic Societies in the Fields of Religion and Theology, University of Stellenbosch, June 2008.

———. "Practical Theology as Part of the Landscape of Social Sciences and Humanities—A Transversal Perspective." *HTS Teologiese Studies* 69:2 (2013) 31–33.

———. "A Post-foundationalist HIV-positive Practical Theology." In *Biennial Conference of the International Academy of Practical Theology.* Proceedings, Brisbane, Australia, 2005.

Bibliography

———. "Transversal Rationality as a Practical Way of Doing Interdisciplinary Work, with HIV and Aids." Proceedings of Seventh International Conference on New Directions in the Humanities, Beijing, China, 2009.

Murphy, Nancey. *Beyond Liberalism and Fundamentalism: How Modern and Postmodern Philosophy Set the Theological Agenda*. New York: Trinity, 2007.

Nel, Malan. *Gemeentebou*. Johannesburg: Orion, 1994.

Nell, Ian A. "Practical Theology as 'Healing of Memories': Critical Reflections on a Specific Methodology." *HTS Teologiese Studies/Theological Studies* 67:2 (2011) 1–8.

Neuman, William Lawrence. *Social Research Methods: Quantitative and Qualitative Approaches*. Boston: Allyn and Bacon, 1994.

Newbigin, Lesslie. *The Gospel in a Pluralist Society*. Grand Rapids: Eerdmans, 1989.

———. *The Open Secret: An Introduction to the Theology of Mission*. Grand Rapids: Eerdmans, 1995.

Niebuhr, H. Richard. *Christ and Culture*. London: Faber & Faber, 1952.

O'Brien, M. R. "Reconciling Identity: Emerging Convictions in Religious Education and Practical Theology." *Religious Education: The Official Journal of the Religious Education Association* 104:3 (May/June 2009) 233–38.

Olson, Roger E. *The Mosaic of Christian Belief: Twenty Centuries of Unity and Diversity*. Downers Grove, IL: InterVarsity, 2002.

Osmer, Richard Robert. *Practical Theology: An Introduction*. Grand Rapids: Eerdmans, 2008.

———. "Toward a Transversal Model of Interdisciplinary Thinking in Practical Theology." In *The Evolution of Rationality: Interdisciplinary Essays in Honor of J. Wentzel Van Huyssteen*, edited by L. R. Schults, 327–45. Grand Rapids: Eerdmans, 2006.

———. "The United States." In *The Wiley-Blackwell Companion to Practical Theology*, edited by Bonnie J. Miller-McLemore, 495–504. Sussex: Blackwell, 2012.

Osmer, Richard Robert, and Friedrich Schweitzer. *Religious Education between Modernization and Globalization: New Perspectives on the United States and Germany*. Grand Rapids: Eerdmans, 2003.

Pannenberg, Wolfhart. *The Apostles' Creed in the Light of Today's Questions*. London: SCM, 1972.

Patomaki, Heikki. *After International Relations: Critical Realism and the (Re)Construction of World Politics*. New York: Routledge, 2002.

Pattison, Stephen. *The Challenge of Practical Theology: Selected Essays*. London: Jessica Kingsley, 2007.

Patton, J. "Introduction to Modern Pastoral Theology in the United States." In *The Blackwell Reader in Pastoral and Practical Theology*, edited by James Woodward and Stephen Pattison, 49–58. Oxford, UK: Blackwell, 2000.

———. *Pastoral Care in Context: An Introduction to Pastoral Care*. Louisville: Westminster John Knox, 1993.

Pierce, Ronald W., Rebecca Merrill Groothuis, and Gordon D. Fee. *Discovering Biblical Equality: Complementarity without Hierarchy*. Downers Grove, IL: InterVarsity, 2004.

Pieterse, H. J. "International Report." *International Journal of Practical Theology* 2 (1998) 155–65.

———. "Die Metode En Metodologie Van Die Praktiese Teologie." In *Eerste Tree in Die Praktiese Teologie*, edited by L. M. Heyns and H. J.C. Pieterse, 66–74. Pretoria, South Africa: Gnosis, 1990.

Bibliography

———. *Praktiese Teologie as Kommunikatiewe Handelingsteorie*. Pretoria, South Africa: RGN-Uitgewers, 1993.

Pillay, G. J., and J. W. Hofmeyr. *Perspectives on Church History: An Introduction for South African Readers*. Pretoria, South Africa: De Jager-HAUM, 1991.

Piper, J. "A Vision of Biblical Complementarity: Manhood and Womanhood Defined According to the Bible." In *Recovering Biblical Manhood and Womanhood: A Response to Evangelical Feminism*, edited by J. Piper and W. Grudem, 31–59. Wheaton: Crossway, 1991.

Poling, James Newton. "Toward a Constructive Practical Theology: A Process-Relational Perspective." *International Journal of Practical Theology* 13:2 (2010) 199–216.

Raeper, William, and Linda Smith. *A Brief Guide to Ideas: Turning Points in the History of Human Thought*. Oxford: Lion, 1991.

Reader, John. *Local Theology: Church and Community in Dialogue*. London: SPCK, 1994.

———. *Reconstructing Practical Theology: The Impact of Globalization*. Hampshire, UK: Ashgate, 2008.

Roberts, J. M. *The New Penguin History of the World*. Camberwell, Australia: Penguin, 2002.

Root, Andrew. "Practical Theology as Social Ethical Action in Christian Ministry: Implications from Emmanuel Levinas and Dietrich Bonhoeffer." *International Journal of Practical Theology* 10:1 (2006) 53–75.

Saayman, W. A. *Christian Mission in South Africa: Political and Ecumenical*. Pretoria, South Africa: University of South Africa, 1991.

Samuel, Vinay, and Chris Sugden. "God's Intention for the World." In *The Church in Response to Human Need*, edited by Vinay Samuel and Chris Sugden, 128–60. Grand Rapids: Regnum, 1987.

Sánchez, Jesús Rodríguez. "The Emerging Field of Pastoral Theology in Puerto Rico." *The Ecumenical Review* 59:2–3 (2007) 221–34.

Sanneh, Lamin O. *Encountering the West: Christianity and the Global Cultural Process: The African Dimension*. Maryknoll, NY: Orbis, 1993.

Schaefer, F. "No Final Conflict." In *The Complete Works of Francis Schaeffer Vol. II: A Christian View of the Bible as Truth*, edited by F. Schaefer, 119–48. Wheaton: Paternoster, 1982.

Schrag, Calvin O. *The Resources of Rationality: A Response to the Postmodern Challenge*. Bloomington, IN: Indiana University Press, 1992.

Schults, F. LeRon. *The Postfoundationalist Task of Theology: Wolfhart Pannenberg and the New Theological Rationality*. Grand Rapids: Eerdmans, 1999.

Schweitzer, F. "Beyond Misunderstanding: The Reality of Practical Theology: A Response to Bonnie J. Miller McLemore from a European Perspective." *International Journal of Practical Theology* 16:1 (2012) 93–103.

Scott, David. *Education, Epistemology and Critical Realism*. New Studies in Critical Realism and Education. New York: Routledge, 2010.

Segundo, Juan Luis. *Liberation of Theology*. Maryknoll, NY: Orbis, 1976.

Shenk, Wilbert R. *Write the Vision: The Church Renewed*. Eugene, OR: Wipf & Stock, 1995.

Southern, R. W. *Western Society and the Church in the Middle Ages*. The Penguin History of the Church 2. London: Penguin, 1970.

Stackhouse, J. G. *Evangelical Futures: A Conversation on Theological Method*. Grand Rapids: Baker, 2000.

Bibliography

Stark, Rodney. *The Rise of Christianity: How the Obscure, Marginal Jesus Movement Became the Dominant Religious Force in the Western World in a Few Centuries*. San Francisco: Harper, 1997.
Stone, H. W., and J. O. Duke. *How to Think Theologically*. Minneapolis: Augsburg, 2006.
Swart, Ignatius. "Meeting the Challenge of Poverty and Exclusion: The Emerging Field of Development Research in South African Practical Theology." *International Journal of Practical Theology* 12:1 (2008) 104–49.
Swinton, John, and Harriet Mowat. *Practical Theology and Qualitative Research*. London: SCM, 2006.
Thiel, John E. *Nonfoundationalism: Guides to Theological Enquiry*. Minneapolis: Fortress, 1994.
Tillich, Paul. *The Courage to Be*. London: Fontana, 1952.
———. *The Shaking of the Foundations*. Victoria, Australia: Penguin, 1949.
Tolstoy, Leo. *War and Peace*. London: Book Club Associates, 1971.
Tracy, David. *The Analogical Imagination: Christian Theology and the Culture of Pluralism*. London: SCM, 1981.
Van der Ven, Johannes A., Jaco S. Dreyer, and Hendrik J.C. Pieterse. "Nature: A Neglected Theme in Practical Theology." *Religion and Theology* 7:1 (2000) 40–55.
Van der Walt, B. J. *Understanding and Rebuilding Africa: From Desperation Today towards Expectation for Tomorrow*. Potchefstroom: Institute for Contemporary Christianity in Africa, 2003.
Van Gelder Craig. *The Ministry of the Missional Church: A Community Led by the Spirit*. Grand Rapids: Baker, 2007.
———. "Mission in the Emerging Post Modern Condition." In *The Church between Gospel and Culture: The Emerging Mission in North America*, edited by G. R. Hunsberger and C. Van Gelder, 113–38. Grand Rapids: Eerdmans, 1996.
Van Huyssteen, Wentzel. *Essays in Postfoundationalist Theology*. Grand Rapids: Eerdmans, 1997.
Van Wyk, A. G. "From 'Applied Theology' to 'Practical Theology.'" *Andrews University Seminary Studies* 33:1 (Spring 1995) 85–101.
Veling, Terry A. *Practical Theology: On Earth as It Is in Heaven*. Maryknoll, NY: Orbis, 2005.
Villa-Vicencio, Charles. *Theology & Violence: The South African Debate*. Grand Rapids: Eerdmans, 1987.
Wakatama, Pius. *Independence for the Third World Church: An African's Perspective on Missionary Work*. Downers Grove, IL: InterVarsity, 1976.
Walls, Jerry L., and Joseph Dongell. *Why I Am Not a Calvinist*. Downers Grove, IL: InterVarsity, 2004.
Ware, Bruce A. "Male and Female Complementarity and the Image of God." In *Biblical Foundations for Manhood and Womanhood*, edited by Wayne Grudem, 71–92. Wheaton: Crossway, 2002.
Ward, P. "The Hermeneutical and Epistemological Significance of Our Students: A Response to Bonnie Miller-Mclemore." *International Journal of Practical Theology* 16:1 (2012) 55–65.
Watson, David. *I Believe in the Church*. London: Hodder & Stoughton, 1978.
Webber, Robert E. *Ancient-Future Faith: Rethinking Evangelicalism for a Postmodern World*. Grand Rapids: Baker Academic, 1999.

Bibliography

Whitehead, James D., and Evelyn Eaton Whitehead. *Method in Ministry: Theological Reflection and Christian Ministry*. Lanham: Sheed & Ward, 1995.

Willows, David, and John Swinton. *Spiritual Dimensions of Pastoral Care: Practical Theology in a Multidisciplinary Context*. London: Kingsley, 2000.

Winston, Robert M. L. *The Story of God: A Personal Journey into the World of Science and Religion*. London: Bantam, 2005.

Wolfteich, Claire. "Animating Questions: Spirituality and Practical Theology." *International Journal of Practical Theology* 13:1 (2009) 121–43.

Woodward, James, and Stephen Pattison, editors. *The Blackwell Reader in Pastoral and Practical Theology*. Oxford: Blackwell, 2000.

Wright, N. T. *The New Testament and the People of God*. London: SPCK, 1992.

———. "The Resurrection: Historical Event or Theological Explanation? A Dialogue." In *The Resurrection of Jesus: John Dominic Crossan and N. T. Wright in Dialogue*, edited by Stewart, 16–47. Minneapolis: Fortress, 2006.

———. *What St Paul Really Said*. Oxford: Lion, 1997.

www.ingramcontent.com/pod-product-compliance
Lightning Source LLC
Chambersburg PA
CBHW050845160426
43192CB00011B/2162